First published in the United Kingdom
by *CHALLENGER PUBLICATIONS* 1996.
ISBN 1 899624 19 8
Copyright Challenger Publications & W.B. Yeadon

LONDON & NORTH EASTERN RAILWAY
LOCOMOTIVE ALLOCATIONS
1st January 1923 (The First Day)

Compiled by W.B. Yeadon

CHALLENGER PUBLICATIONS
15 Lovers Lane
Grasscroft
Oldham OL4 4DP

(above) This is the Great Eastern's no.1 as seen on the FIRST DAY, <u>and</u> because it was also ex Stratford works in October 1923 from a general repair, without alteration to its painting. Date of photograph is 23rd May 1925, so it would keep this pre-Grouping style until it again went to works for repair in December 1925.

Printed & bound by
Haslam Printers Ltd
Chorley

CHALLENGER PUBLICATIONS

INTRODUCTION

My first venture as a solo author concerning LNER locomotives was published in September 1989, and it described where all 6815 of them were allocated on the last day of that Company's existence. The LNER came into being exactly 25 years previously, as a result of the Railways Act of 1921 ordering that five large, and two smaller companies be grouped into one homogenous organisation, which then adopted the title of London & North Eastern Railway Company. Its constituents were the Great Northern, the Great Central, the Great Eastern, the North British, the Great North of Scotland, and the North Eastern Railways. Pre-empting the larger move, the latter and the Hull & Barnsley Railway had amalgamated with effect from 1st April 1922.

So, from 12.01 a.m. on 1st January 1923, the new L&NER became the owner of 7392 steam locomotives, plus another 17 regarded as in Departmental use, i.e. non-revenue earning. They were allocated to 148 sheds ranging from Elgin to London and Wrexham to Yarmouth. Today, you need to be well into your eighties to have any personal memory of that event, and those who have such recollection are rapidly reducing in number. Surprisingly, there is growing demand from modellers for accurate, and comprehensive information to enable them to display, and/or operate their layouts and rolling stock, at a level which obviates criticism.

Having trained as a mechanical engineer, I acquired the facility for assembling and presenting facts tidily, leading to professional employment on catalogue preparation, culminating in changing a 420-page handbook from Imperial to metric dimensions. The listing of thousands of figures for dates and dimensions applicable to LNER locomotives was thus merely extension of daily work, but with the important difference of being done for pleasure.

Putting together the data for Allocations on the Last Day posed no problem, because by 1947 railway enthusiast societies had been accepted, and given official recognition, even full co-operation by staff at senior levels. To do the same allocations at the end of 1922 was a very different matter. Organised enthusiasts were limited to the very small number then members of the Stephenson Locomotive Society, or in The Railway Club, and for information, one had to depend on (and be able to afford) either The Railway Magazine, or The Railway Gazette. Certainly there was nothing published concerning shed allocations, other than from where an engine under mention was working. Thus I need to explain how this account was compiled.

In the mid-1930s I became a member of The Railway Correspondence & Travel Society and was also elected a member of the Stephenson Locomotive Society, of both of which I am still in membership. By then, both Societies had matured sufficiently to be in regular receipt of official shed allocations and of transfers between sheds. Complete allocations for all LNER sheds as at 1st January

1933 were available in printed form, so with that as a basis, I needed to find what alterations had taken place in the previous ten years. For North Eastern Area I had the extreme good fortune (when steam was being phased out) to be given a ledger which had been the daily record maintained in the office of the Locomotive Running Superintendent at York from the beginning of 1925. For the majority of transfers between sheds, a brief mention of why they had been made was also entered. Because most engines in that Area retained their original number when they became LNER stock, the individual Engine History Cards from before the Grouping continued to be used, and when those *were* superseded, many had been lodged with the Archivist in the Headquarters building at York. They showed transfers made during the years 1923 and 1924 in that Area, which left only engines withdrawn in those two years to be located. For those, the Works Manager's Office at Darlington came to my rescue, because they gave me an old hand-written ledger, in which withdrawals had been listed as they took place. Not only was date of withdrawal entered but also the name of the shed to which the engine had been allocated. For good measure, that register also listed age of engine and of the boiler, and tender, the type of brake, and if steam heating had been fitted, whether it was complete, or just at the back end. It had been started in 1906, and the final entry was 21st March 1951, a note stating "M.E. office record discontinued from March 1951 when office closed". Also listed are the engines sold to private firms for those same 45 years: treasure trove indeed. Apart from any late transfers in 1923/4, I could rest content that I had reasonably complete coverage of N.E. Area stock.

In Southern Area, for running purposes, there was division into Western (GN and GC) and Eastern (GE) Sections. Maintenance for Western was done mainly by Doncaster and Gorton works, whilst Stratford did that for Eastern Section engines. Each of those works recorded it on Form C.M.E. 9018 for individual engines, but the shed to which each engine was allocated kept card L.R. 7759 as their readily available record. My diligent and persistent search, taking about forty years, eventually located the majority of those cards for engines which were in stock subsequent to January 1925. The 9018 and 7759 series had been started when an engine had been given its LNER numbering from February 1924 onwards. They provided allocation from that date, and any later transfers, but quite a number of cards showed the date when the engine had first arrived at the shed making out the card, although pre-Grouping on many of them. Just how luck affected research is well illustrated by my discovering that cards made out for Austerity 2-8-0 engines built during the 1939-45 war, had been in previous use for engines withdrawn during the years 1935 to 1939. Those 7759 cards had not been discarded, and the wartime paper shortage led to their reverse side being brought into use, providing me with unexpected information.

Doncaster works were alone in including 'No.' for the lowest number they used. This one ceased to carry it after it went for repair on 21st March 1923. *W.H.Whitworth.*

At the northern extremity of LNER territory, the Great North of Scotland's engine had it's No.1 on a cast plate, as here at Kittybrewster.

I was also greatly indebted to two LNER enthusiasts, both sadly long departed. Alfred Croughton was the source of Southern Area weekly transfer sheets for 1928/29/30, and Eric Neve provided me with copies of similar data back to 1925, which the clerk at Top Shed had given him. Those filled in many gaps, but also confirmed many card entries, making me reasonably content that Southern Area allocations were as near completion as could be expected forty years later.

Scottish Area proved to be the weakest link. Their official allocation as at 1st January 1933 had been circulated, and I located a copy of it, together with subsequent transfers. But no 7759 cards for engines already withdrawn by then ever came to my notice, so dates of moves in the 1923-32 years are lacking. However, doom and gloom anent them is to some extent offset because, at that time, some Edinburgh based enthusiasts took every opportunity of talking their way into LNER sheds in Scotland, and were persistent and meticulous recorders. The names of Boyd, Rutherford, Robertson, Stephen (R.D. and W.D.M.), Findlater, and Hermiston should be gratefully remembered for you and I now knowing where North British and G.N.of S. engines were shedded when they became LNER owned. To those names must be added that of a slightly younger Hennigan, whose enthusiasm for N.B. led to his gathering together the data from his elders, and also to my being privileged to have access to it.

ITEMS OF CONSEQUENCE

The "LAST DAY ALLOCATIONS" published in September 1989 perforce used the numbers the engines then carried, but during 1946, the complete locomotive stock had been re-numbered into a less random arrangement. Unless that radical change is taken into account, there is no connection between what each engine was numbered on the FIRST, and on the LAST day of the LNER.

The running numbers used in this publication are what each engine had on 1st January 1923, so with contributions from seven constituents, there was considerable duplication. For example, no.1 could be seen on seven very different locomotives, because although the Hull & Barnsley's no.1 had been taken out of stock in April 1922 (so was not owned by the LNER), it could still be seen derelict outside Hull Springhead shed until June 1923, when they finally got around to cutting up that 1884 built 0-6-0 tank engine which still had its original boiler. The Great Northern actually had two no.1's (three if the Stirling Single is taken into account), a 0-6-0 mixed traffic tender engine, and also a 0-4-0 tank engine portion of a steam railmotor. On the Great Central it was carried by a large 2-8-0 goods tender, and the cover picture shows the 2-4-2 passenger tank engine from the Great Eastern. The North British also used no.1 for a passenger tank engine but a 4-4-2 type, and on the Great North of Scotland it was a 4-4-0 tender engine built in 1878. Until January 1914 the North Eastern also had two no.1's, a 4-4-0 tender engine built in 1887, which was then changed to no.356 to avoid confusion with electric 0-4-4-0 no.1

built in 1905. Not until Group numbering was introduced in February 1924 was duplication of numbering eliminated.

The main workshops at Doncaster and at Darlington began preparations in November 1922 to recognise that their Company titles had only brief life left to them, but they were then quite unaware of what change would be required. So, Doncaster simply ceased applying GNR by transfers on to tenders, 4-4-0 no.1346, and 4-4-2 no.1429 being sent out without that indication of ownership. From Darlington, where tenders carried only NORTH (armorial) EASTERN on each side, that was altered to N.E.R. and, instead of the armorial, the number of the engine was displayed. 2-4-0 no.1479, 4-4-0 no.2106, and two 4-4-2's nos. 2168 and 2169 were so changed, before Group Standard livery and numbering style was promulgated.

For each shed the full list of engines allocated to it at 1st January 1923 is shown, but it needs to be appreciated that others of similar class may have been transferred there on a temporary basis to cover for absence of engines away at the workshops for repair. That was normal procedure, especially at the smaller sheds, where their own reserves were limited. Another factor to be taken into account applied particularly to Great Northern sheds, because their allocations were to Districts, and not specifically to sheds in the District. Taking London District as an example, King's Cross ("Top Shed") was the main shed, but had the responsibility for keeping Hornsey, Hatfield, Hitchin and Cambridge sheds adequately supplied. Similarly, whilst Ardsley was the key shed for West Riding District, it had to make sure that Bradford, and Leeds (Copley Hill) had enough engines for duties covered by those two sheds. Not until well into LNER years were most sheds given their own definite allocations. So, in 1923 it was no surprise to a commuter from Hitchin if, for some weeks, his morning train to town was regularly hauled by an engine ostensibly allocated to another shed in London District.

THE L N E R LOCOMOTIVE CLASSIFICATION

This is where I am going to claim "Author's Privilege" to step out of line slightly. On FIRST DAY the new Company understandably had not got around to formulating a comprehensive system for easy identification of the 240 different classes of locomotives it had acquired. If I was to refer you to J16, 5A, C72, G3, 290, F, and E classes, few would be aware that they all applied to 0-6-0 tank type. But by changing them into J55, J63, J68, J75, J77, J88 and J91 you (like me) would readily recognise them as coming from - respectively - Great Northern, Great Central, Great Eastern, Hull & Barnsley, North Eastern, North British, and Great North of Scotland Railways.

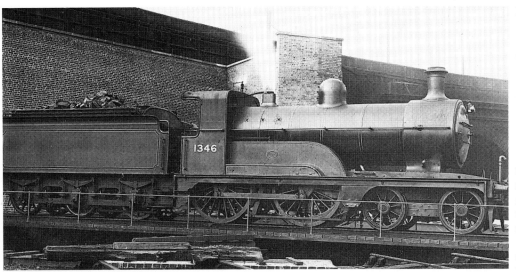

Thus, I make no apology for using in FIRST DAY the system devised by the legendary 'Teddy' Windle in Doncaster Drawing Office, to which Gresley gave his approval on 3rd September 1923. As it did for LNER employees, it makes it easy for you to understand the headings that I have used for each class, and for me to present a tidy arrangement. For the younger generation, not lucky enough to do their study of LNER locomotives when that nomenclature was second nature to their more fortunate fellow enthusiasts, I would refer them for more detailed, or dimensional and technical information on every class to the 19 volumes (the 'Green Books') which the Railway Correspondence & Travel Society published under the title *Locomotives of the LNER* from July 1963 and completed in November 1994. For those more interested in the layout of sheds, and the actual facilities they provided for the locomotives allocated to them, a variety of books have been published. *Great Northern Engine Sheds* by Griffiths and Hooper is typical, and recommended reading for those aspects of our hobby.

DEPARTMENTAL LOCOMOTIVES

In addition to those in capital stock, some of the LNER's constituent companies had engines specifically allocated for use at the workshops, and so regarded as non-revenue earning. Attitude differed as to how they were counted in the total stock returns. The Great Central, North British and the Great North of Scotland claimed no Departmental locomotives, their totals of 1358, 1074 and 122 respectively all being running stock. The North British did however have one petrol engined shunter of which their return took no account. The Great Northern capital stock was 1359, but they also had two Departmentals, a 0-4-4 crane tank at Doncaster works, and a 0-6-0 tank used by the sleeper creosoting works near Boston. Both survived Grouping by some years, but neither was ever accorded an LNER classification, and both were single examples of their type.

The Great Eastern recorded seven as Departmental Stock, in addition to their 1336 in capital stock. Three were 0-6-0 crane tanks (all similar) used at Stratford works, and to which the LNER later gave class J92. Another (no.281) also used at Stratford was one out of a class of 50, the other 49 being in capital stock. At that works were also three 0-4-0 tank engines, two ancient small ones numbered 230 and 0228 substantially alike, but also a much more powerful one built as recently as January 1921, and of which four similar were in capital stock. That constituent also possessed an un-numbered petrol shunter used in the Engineer's yard at Lowestoft, of the same type as that on the North British, which they did not include in their

totals. Much later, the LNER numbered that pair as 8430/31 and gave them class Y11, and both served to take up British Railways numbering.

The North Eastern Railway contributed no less than 2143 locomotives to capital, plus 13 electrics and also 8 Departmentals. Three of the latter, 0-6-0 tank no.263, and 0-4-0 tank nos. 129 and 898, served Darlington works; two, 0-6-0 crane tank no.995 and 0-6-0 tank no.1662, were used similarly by Gateshead works, and the other crane tank no.590 worked at Percy Main scrapyard. The eight also included two 2-2-4 tank engines, no.66 based at Darlington, and no.190 kept at Heaton, both used for hauling Officers' inspection saloons.

NUMBERING OF DUPLICATE STOCK

For accountancy purposes concerned with additions to capital stock, or replacements charged to revenue, the LNER's constituents adopted various procedures. To identify an engine which was being superseded, but which was not being considered for early withdrawal, and whose number was being used for a newly built engine, the Great Northern, and the Great North of Scotland, simply appended the letter A. That led to some interesting pairs, as the following example shows. the big 2-6-0 type which Gresley introduced in March 1920 were given numbers 1000 to 1009, of which 1001 to 1008 were readily available, because the engines which had carried them had been scrapped by February 1916. No.1000 was still occupied by a 2-4-0 built in 1895, so on 16th February 1920, that engine's number had A added to it, the FIRST DAY entry for it being 1000A. It was then withdrawn from stock on 4th January 1924 and cut up in November 1924, which cleared the duplication. But a 4-4-2 tank built in February 1898, and then numbered 1009 proved much tougher after it became 1009A in August 1921. That GNR 1009A became LNER 1009A from March 1926 which it carried for more than twenty years, until on 22nd December 1946 it was changed to 7350 in the Thompson re-numbering scheme. Even longer in A stock was 0-6-0 goods tank no.155 built in august 1897 and carrying the A from November 1906 until re-numbered 8804 on 17th November 1946. Both those veterans were then in British Railways stock until withdrawn in April and October 1955.

'A' stock on the Great North of Scotland had a very different experience. When its 52A was withdrawn on 26th January 1926 it was the last with an A, and none of the seven with A which became LNER property acquired that Company's numbering or livery.

The Hull & Barnsley had also used the A addition for its Duplicate Stock, but the 25 carrying it at the April 1922 amalgamation with the North eastern, had all been withdrawn later that year, so never concerned the LNER. Rather curiously, the North Eastern was the only one of the constituents not to have any locomotives carrying Duplicate Stock numbering.

(above) **Darlington also confined their first attempt at change to tenders, reducing the full Company name to just initials, and the engine's number was added to take the place of the now redundant armorial.**

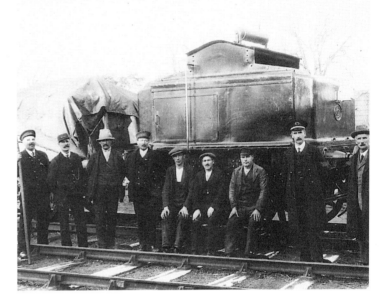

(right) **PETROL ENGINE No.1 - so limned - would be on holiday on FIRST DAY, because in Scotland they observed New Year's Day as such, and it was Kelso's goods yard shunter. The North British did not include this item in its stock return.**

On the Great Central the letter B was appended to the number when an engine was transferred to their Duplicate Stock, that procedure being continued until as far into LNER as early February 1924. The 0-6-0 goods engine 483 built in August 1882 was the last to have B added, so as to avoid conflicting with the 4-cylinder 4-6-0 new on 2nd February 1924 which was given number 483. Then the ex-G.C. duplicates acquired a respectability not accorded to any of the others in the Group, because in the "all-line" numbering scheme effective from February 1924, all the letter B's were allocated numbers from 6402 to 6494 in running stock. Not all of them survived however to have them applied, although 6408 to 6411 did manage to participate in the 1946 re-numbering.

The Great Eastern provided other variations, because for their duplicates they used a figure 0 as a prefix to the number. 0-6-0 tender engines 38 and 39 built in April 1884 still carried those numbers on FIRST DAY, but in November 1923 became 038 and 039 because new 0-6-0 tank engines had been given 31 to 40. Both the tender engines duly got 07038 and 07039 and survived long enough to have them transferred from tender to cab side. The Great Eastern also had three 0-6-0 crane tanks, regarded as Departmental Stock, but carrying B, C, and D instead of numbering, which persisted until they took 8667/8/9 in the 1946 re-numbering. Letter A had been carried by a 0-4-0 saddle tank locomotive used by Stratford works, which only failed to make LNER ownership by about a year.

The remaining constituent, the North British, made transfers to their Duplicate List by numbering them consecutively from 1001 upwards, and had reached 1471 by the end of 1921. No additions were made in 1922, but that system was continued briefly in LNER days because in January-March 1923, ten 0-6-0's built in 1881 and numbered 519 to 528 were given 1472 to 1481. The LNER addition of 9000 to ex-N.B. numbers put the duplicates into five-figure numbering which survived until 17th November 1946 when two 0-4-0 tanks changed from 10094 and 10101 to 8095 and 8092 respectively.

Authors note: The first part of the book lists the individual locomotives in their repective classes with a shed code alongside. The second section lists the sheds and their allocations.

SHED CODES BY GROUP CONSTITUENTS

GREAT CENTRAL 1358

ANN	Annesley	80
BRN	Barnsley	43
BID	Bidston	7
CHR	Chester	12
GOR	Gorton	178
IMM	Immingham	101
KDY	Keadby	19
LNG	Langwith	61
LEI	Leicester	26
LIN	Lincoln	36
LIV	Liverpool (Brunswick)	54
MEX	Mexborough	170
NEA	Neasden	69
NWH	New Holland	10
NTH	Northwich	35
RET	Retford	44
SHF	Sheffield	108
STV	Staveley	47
STP	Stockport	47
TFD	Trafford Park	63
TUX	Tuxford	16
WAL	Walton (Liverpool)	33
WIG	Wigan	15
WFD	Woodford	48
WRX	Wrexham	36

GREAT EASTERN 1336

CAM	Cambridge	178
COL	Colchester	47
DON	Doncaster	5
IPS	Ipswich	131
KL	King's Lynn	37
LIN	Lincoln	12
LOW	Lowestoft	22
MAR	March	97
NOR	Norwich	119
PKS	Parkeston	20
PBE	Peterborough East	86
STR	Stratford	555
WIS	Wisbech	7
YAR	Yarmouth	20

GREAT NORTHERN 1359

ARD	Ardsley	94
BOS	Boston	62
BFD	Bradford	90
CAM	Cambridge (GN)	10
CLK	Colwick	231
COP	Copley Hill	43
DON	Doncaster	189
GRA	Grantham	67
HAT	Hatfield	29
HIT	Hitchin	28
HSY	Hornsey	76
KX	King's Cross	156

LEI	Leicester	5
LIN	Lincoln	32
LTH	Louth	8
NWE	New England	180
RET	Retford	30
TFD	Manchester	15
YK	York	14

GREAT NORTH OF SCOTLAND 122

ELG	Elgin	14
KEI	Keith	14
KIT	Kittybrewster	94

NORTH BRITISH 1074

ABD	Aberdeen	19
BGT	Bathgate	59
BLA	Blaydon	2
BWK	Berwick	27
BTD	Burntisland	30
CAR	Carlisle (Canal)	39
DFU	Dunfermline	51
DEE	Dundee	78
EFD	Eastfield	181
HAW	Hawick	21
HAY	Haymarket	50
HEX	Hexham	1
KPS	Kipps	71
PKD	Parkhead	56
PTH	Perth	24
POL	Polmont	44
RDS	Reedsmouth	5
Roth	Rothbury	2
STG	Stirling	25
STM	St Margarets	213
THJ	Thornton Junction	75

NORTH EASTERN 2143

ALN	Alnmouth	11
ALS	Alston	1
ANP	Annfield Plain	8
BCas	Barnard Castle	8
BLA	Blaydon	69
BOR	Borough Gardens	65
BOW	Bowes Bridge	3
BFD	Bradford (Manningham)	1
BRI	Bridlington	7
BCJ	Bullcroft Junction	4
CAR	Carlisle (London Rd)	49
CON	Consett	2
CUD	Cudworth	30
DAR	Darlington	83
DEN	Denaby	2
DON	Doncaster (GN)	2
DUR	Durham	7
EHL	East Hartlepool	36
FYL	Ferryhill	28

GHD	Gateshead	105
GSB	Guisborough	1
HAV	Haverton Hill	13
HawJ	Hawes Junction	2
HAY	Haymarket (NE)	4
HTN	Heaton	130
HEX	Hexham	5
HLA	Hull Alexandra Dock	24
HLB	Hull Botanic Gardens	47
HLD	Hull Dairycoates	146
HLS	Hull Springhead	120
KBS	Kirkby Stephen	14
MAL	Malton	18
MAS	Masham	1
MID	Middlesbrough	62
MinT	Middleton-in-Teesdale	1
NEV	Neville Hill	82
NPT	Newport	90
NMN	Normanton	4
NLT	Northallerton	9
NBH	North Blyth	28
PatB	Pateley Bridge	1
PEL	Pelton Level	2
PEN	Penrith	1
PMN	Percy Main	33
PKG	Pickering	4
Rich	Richmond	1
ROS	Rosedale	3
SALT	Saltburn	16
SCA	Scarborough	27
SEL	Selby	57
SDN	Shildon	59
SBH	South Blyth	28
STH	Stanhope	1
SBK	Starbeck	50
SKN	Stockton	47
SUN	Sunderland	81
THK	Thirsk	14
TWD	Tweedmouth	44
TDK	Tyne Dock	93
WAS	Waskerley	9
WRH	Wearhead	1
WVJ	Wear Valley Junction	4
WAuk	West Auckland	23
WHL	West Hartlepool	77
WBY	Whitby	17
YK	York	129

Note: The above codes are by no means the **official** **codes** used by either the LNER or any of the companies that formed the railway in 1923. Similar coding was in use at various periods but those listed here are simply reproduced to help the reader identify the following listings.

Numbers to the right of the shed name indicate how many locomotives were allocated to the shed as at 1/1/23.

GCR 1358

A5 (21)

23	NEA
24	NEA
128	NEA
129	NEA
165	NEA
166	NEA
167	NEA
168	NEA
169	NEA
170	NEA
371	NEA
372	NEA
373	NEA
374	NEA
411	NEA
447	NEA
448	NEA
449	NEA
450	NEA
451	NEA
452	NEA

B1 (2)

195	GOR
196	IMM

B2 (6)

423	GOR
424	GOR
425	GOR
426	GOR
427	GOR
428	GOR

B3 (6)

1164	GOR
1165	GOR
1166	GOR
1167	GOR
1168	GOR
1169	GOR

B4 (10)

1095	SHF
1096	SHF
1097	SHF
1098	SHF
1099	SHF
1100	SHF
1101	SHF
1102	SHF
1103	SHF
1104	SHF

B5 (14)

180	IMM
181	IMM
182	IMM
183	IMM
184	IMM
185	GOR
186	MEX
187	LIN
1067	MEX
1068	MEX
1069	MEX
1070	MEX
1071	MEX
1072	MEX

B6 (3)

52	GOR
53	GOR
416	GOR

B7 (28)

31	LEI
32	LEI
33	LEI
34	GOR
35	GOR
36	IMM
37	IMM
38	IMM
72	GOR
73	GOR
78	GOR
458	NEA
459	NEA
460	NEA
461	NEA
462	WFD
463	NEA
464	NEA
465	SHF
466	SHF
467	WFD
468	WFD
469	WFD
470	GOR
471	GOR
472	GOR
473	GOR
474	GOR

B8 (11)

4	ANN
279	ANN
280	GOR
439	GOR
440	ANN
441	ANN
442	GOR
443	GOR
444	GOR
445	GOR
446	ANN

B9 (10)

1105	LIN
1106	GOR
1107	LIN
1108	LIN
1109	GOR
1110	GOR
1111	LIN
1112	LIN
1113	GOR
1114	GOR

C4 (27)

192	LEI
194	WFD
260	WFD
261	WFD
262	WFD
263	WFD
264	LEI
265	LEI
266	LEI
267	LEI
358	LEI
360	LEI
361	LEI
362	WFD
363	LEI
1083	LEI
1084	WFD
1085	WAL
1086	LEI
1087	LEI
1088	WFD
1089	LEI
1090	LEI
1091	WFD
1092	LEI
1093	WFD
1094	WFD

C5 (4)

258	LEI
259	LEI
364	LEI
365	LEI

C13 (40)

2	CHR
9	CHR
18	TFD
20	STP
27	TFD
28	WRX
29	TFD
47	CHR
50	TFD
55	CHR
114	TFD
115	WRX
171	WRX
178	WRX
179	TFD
188	WRX
190	WRX
191	TFD
193	CHR
199	MEX
310	CHR
357	TFD
359	WRX
453	WRX
454	WRX
455	WRX
456	TFD
457	CHR
1055	SHF
1056	SHF
1057	SHF
1058	RET
1059	SHF
1060	SHF
1061	SHF
1062	SHF
1063	SHF
1064	MEX
1065	SHF
1066	SHF

C14 (12)

1120	LNG
1121	LNG
1122	ANN
1123	LNG
1124	ANN
1125	NEA
1126	WFD
1127	ANN
1128	ANN
1129	ANN
1130	STP
1131	STP

D5 (6)

694	WAL
695	WAL
696	WAL
697	WAL
698	WAL
699	WAL

D6 (33)

268	LIV
269	WAL
270	LIV
852	TFD
853	TFD
854	TFD
855	TFD
856	TFD
857	TFD
858	TFD
859	LIV
860	TFD
861	TFD
862	LIV
863	LIV
864	LIV
865	TFD
866	TFD
867	TFD
868	TFD
869	LIV
870	TFD
871	LIV
872	TFD
873	TFD
874	TFD
875	TFD
876	TFD
877	LIV
878	LIV
879	LIV
880	LIV
881	LIV

D7 (31)

561	IMM
562	LIN
563	MEX
564	LIN
565	SHF
566	IMM
567	IMM
682	IMM
683	SHF
684	NWH
685	IMM
686	IMM
687	IMM
688	MEX
689	MEX
690	MEX
691	MEX
692	MEX
693	SHF
700	LIN
701	NTH
702	NTH
703	NTH
704	NTH
705	LIN
706	NWH
707	NTH
708	IMM
709	NTH
710	BRN
711	NWH

D8 (3)

508B	WAL
510B	WAL
511B	WAL

D9 (40)

104	RET
105	RET
106	SHF
107	RET
108	SHF
109	SHF
110	LIV
111	SHF
112	MEX
113	LIN
1013	LIN
1014	SHF
1015	SHF
1016	ANN
1017	LIV
1018	IMM
1019	SHF
1020	SHF
1021	LIN
1022	ANN
1023	ANN
1024	LIN
1025	ANN
1026	SHF
1027	SHF
1028	ANN
1029	SHF
1030	SHF
1031	SHF
1032	SHF
1033	ANN
1034	SHF
1035	ANN
1036	LIN
1037	SHF
1038	ANN
1039	ANN
1040	SHF
1041	SHF
1042	SHF

D10 (10)

429	NEA
430	GOR
431	GOR
432	NEA
433	GOR
434	GOR
435	GOR
436	GOR
437	NEA
438	GOR

D11 (11)

501	NEA
502	NEA
503	NEA
504	NEA
505	NEA
506	NEA
507	NEA
508	NEA
509	NEA
510	NEA
511	NEA

D12 (12)

128B	NWH
423B	LIV
425B	GOR
428B	ANN
430B	LIV
434B	GOR
439B	NWH
440B	STV
441B	TFD
442B	ANN
443B	ANN
446B	LIV

12A (1)

169B	ANN

E2 (3)

506B	WAL
507B	LIN
509B	LIN

E8 (2)

449B	NEA
450B	NEA

F1 (39)

574	GOR
575	GOR
576	GOR
577	GOR
578	STP
579	STP
580	GOR
581	STP
582	GOR
583	GOR
584	GOR
585	GOR
586	STP
587	GOR
588	GOR
589	GOR
590	STP
591	STP
592	STP
593	STP
594	GOR
595	GOR
596	GOR
597	STP
598	STP
599	STP
600	STP
726	GOR
727	GOR
728	GOR
729	GOR
730	GOR
731	GOR
732	GOR
733	GOR
734	GOR
735	GOR
736	GOR
737	GOR

F2 (10)

776	GOR
777	LIV
778	LIV
779	LIV
780	LIV
781	LIV
782	LIV
783	WAL
784	GOR
785	LIV

G3 (6)

1148B	LNG
1149B	LNG
1150B	LNG
1151B	LNG
1152B	LNG
1169B	LNG

J8 (12)

549	STV
550	STV
551	STV
552	STV
553	STV
554	STV
555	STV
556	STV
557	STV
558	STV
559	STV
560	STV

J9 (31)

645	NTH
646	NTH
647	NTH
648	GOR
649	NTH
650	NTH
651	GOR
652	NTH
653	NTH
654	NTH
655	NTH
656	NTH
657	NTH
658	NTH
659	GOR
660	NTH
661	NTH
662	NTH
663	NTH
664	GOR
665	NTH
666	NTH
667	NTH
668	NTH
669	NTH
738	NTH
739	NTH
740	NTH
741	NTH
742	NTH
743	NTH

J10 (124)

74	MEX
75	MEX
76	WAL
77	MEX
79	WAL
80	WAL
81	WAL
82	WAL
83	WAL
84	WAL
90	LIV
94	LIV
95	LIV
96	LIV
97	LIV
98	STP
99	WAL
100	WAL
101	LIV
103	WAL
116	STP
117	STP
118	LIV
119	STP
120	STP
121	STP
122	STP
123	WAL
124	STP
125	WAL
126	STP
130	STP
131	STP
132	STP
134	GOR
141	LIV
172	LIV
174	LIV
175	LIV
176	LIV
639	SHF
640	SHF
641	NTH
642	SHF
643	SHF
644	NTH
670	SHF
671	BRN
672	SHF
673	SHF
674	SHF
675	SHF
676	SHF
677	SHF
678	SHF
679	SHF
680	SHF
681	SHF
786	IMM
787	RET
788	TFD
789	RET
790	RET
791	RET
792	RET
793	RET
794	RET
795	RET
796	ANN
797	IMM
798	TFD
799	RET
800	IMM
801	TFD
802	RET
803	TFD
804	TFD
805	IMM
806	IMM
807	LIV
808	NWH
809	NWH
810	LIV
811	TFD
812	TFD
813	RET
814	SHF
815	TFD
816	ANN
817	IMM
818	RET
819	IMM
820	STP
821	RET
822	RET
823	NWH
824	STP
825	STP
826	STP
827	NWH
828	RET
829	STP
830	STP
831	RET
832	RET
833	STP
834	STP
835	ANN
836	STP
837	IMM
838	IMM
839	STP
840	IMM
841	IMM
842	WRX
843	STP
844	IMM
845	RET
846	IMM
847	RET
848	GOR
849	ANN
850	ANN
851	RET

J11 (174)

16	SHF
177	LIN
197	WFD
198	WFD
201	WFD
202	GOR
203	LEI
204	LNG
205	LEI
206	MEX
207	WFD
208	GOR
209	WFD
210	GOR
211	GOR
214	WFD
215	WFD
216	WFD
217	LNG
218	LNG
219	WFD
220	LIN
221	NEA
222	LNG
223	LNG
224	GOR
225	GOR
226	GOR
227	ANN
228	WFD
229	LNG
230	RET
231	RET
232	GOR
233	WFD
234	GOR
235	GOR
236	GOR
237	GOR
238	WFD
239	LNG
240	LNG
241	WFD
242	GOR
243	ANN
244	ANN
245	GOR
246	LNG
247	GOR
248	LIN
249	RET
250	NEA
252	WFD
253	LIN
254	RET
255	GOR
256	LNG
257	LNG
281	WFD
282	NEA
283	RET
284	RET
285	NEA
286	RET
287	RET
288	LNG
289	GOR
290	GOR
291	GOR
292	ANN
293	LIN
294	ANN
295	RET
296	RET
297	WFD
298	NEA
299	LIN
300	LIN
301	SHF
302	ANN
303	GOR
304	RET
305	SHF
306	ANN
307	LIV
308	LIN
309	MEX
311	LIN
312	LNG
313	GOR
314	LIN
315	LIN
316	GOR
317	LNG
318	LNG
319	GOR
320	WFD
322	LIN

323	WFD	1050	WFD	494	MEX	413B	MEX	343	ANN	712	STV
324	RET	1051	WFD	495	WIG	414B	IMM	344	WFD	713	STV
325	WFD	1078	GOR	496	WIG	415B	IMM	345	ANN	714	BRN
326	ANN	1079	RET	497	TFD	417B	MEX	366	LNG	715	STV
327	ANN	1080	LNG	498	TFD	418B	LIV	367	NEA	716	SHF
328	ANN	1081	NEA	499	TFD	420B	GOR	368	WFD	717	STV
329	ANN	1082	NEA	500	TFD	421B	ANN	369	WFD	718	BRN
330	SHF	1115	LIN	501B	WIG			370	ANN	719	BRN
947	SHF	1116	LIN	502B	WIG	**J60** (4)				720	STV
948	LNG	1117	RET	503B	TFD			**M1** (9)		721	SHF
949	SHF	1118	LIN	504B	WIG	1153B	LNG			722	SHF
950	SHF	1119	RET	505B	WAL	1154B	LNG	1145	TUX	723	MEX
951	GOR					1155B	LNG	1146	LNG	724	BRN
952	TFD	**J12** (61)		**J13** (6)		1156B	LNG	1147	TUX	725	BRN
953	SHF							1148	TUX		
954	SHF	3B	WIG	568	MEX	**J61** (2)		1149	TUX	**N5** (129)	
955	GOR	6	WIG	569	MEX			1150	TUX		
973	IMM	7	MEX	570	BRN	278	IMM	1151	TUX	21	BRN
974	IMM	30B	MEX	571	MEX	407B	IMM	1152	TUX	25	BRN
975	IMM	31B	MEX	572	MEX			1153	TUX	51	MEX
976	IMM	32B	MEX	573	MEX	**J62** (12)				54	BRN
977	IMM	34B	MEX					**N4** (55)		127	BRN
978	IMM	35B	MEX	**'18'** (1)		882	BID			173	MEX
979	IMM	36B	TFD			883	WRX	512	STV	189	BRN
980	IMM	37B	TFD	309B	GOR W	884	BID	513	STV	200	BRN
981	IMM	38B	MEX			885	IMM	514	BRN	251	BRN
982	IMM	45	TFD	**J58** (14)		886	BID	601	SHF	409	WRX
983	IMM	46	WIG			887	IMM	602	SHF	410	WRX
984	IMM	458B	MEX	5B	TFD	888	WRX	603	STV	515	BRN
985	IMM	459B	TFD	8B	BID	889	IMM	604	SHF	516	MEX
986	IMM	460B	MEX	22B	GOR	890	STV	605	SHF	517	MEX
987	IMM	461B	TFD	41B	IMM	891	WRX	606	SHF	518	GOR
988	IMM	462B	MEX	52B	GOR	892	BID	607	SHF	519	GOR
989	IMM	463B	MEX	53B	GOR	893	WRX	608	SHF	520	GOR
990	IMM	464B	TFD	66B	LNG			609	STV	521	BRN
991	GOR	465B	MEX	72B	BID	**J63** (7)		610	STV	522	GOR
992	IMM	466B	TFD	73B	RET			611	SHF	523	GOR
993	GOR	467B	MEX	78B	WRX	60	IMM	612	SHF	524	GOR
994	IMM	468B	MEX	88	LIN	61	IMM	613	BRN	525	GOR
995	IMM	469B	TFD	154	LIN	89	NWH	614	STV	526	GOR
996	IMM	470B	TFD	156	BID	157	LIV	615	STV	527	GOR
997	IMM	471B	WIG	158	NEA	277	IMM	616	STV	528	GOR
998	IMM	472B	WIG			321	IMM	617	SHF	529	GOR
999	IMM	473B	WIG	**J59** (26)		538	LIV	618	STV	530	WRX
1000	IMM	474B	WIG					619	SHF	531	WRX
1001	IMM	475	MEX	272B	IMM	**'7'** (2)		620	LIN	532	GOR
1002	IMM	476	MEX	273B	IMM			621	LNG	533	BRN
1003	GOR	477	MEX	274B	MEX	10B	WRX	622	SHF	534	GOR
1004	GOR	478	TFD	275B	GOR	11B	WRX	623	BRN	535	GOR
1005	IMM	479	TFD	276B	GOR			624	STV	536	GOR
1006	IMM	480	WIG	277B	MEX	**L1** (20)		625	STV	537	GOR
1007	IMM	481	MEX	279B	IMM			626	SHF	539	WRX
1008	IMM	482	WIG	280B	IMM	272	IMM	627	SHF	540	GOR
1009	LIN	483	WIG	336B	LIV	273	ANN	628	SHF	541	GOR
1010	IMM	484	TFD	338B	STP	274	ANN	629	BRN	542	GOR
1011	IMM	485	MEX	339B	STP	275	GOR	630	BRN	543	GOR
1012	IMM	486	MEX	340B	SHF	276	NEA	631	SHF	544	BRN
1043	WFD	487	MEX	342B	STP	336	NEA	632	SHF	545	MEX
1044	WFD	488	MEX	367B	IMM	337	ANN	633	SHF	546	BRN
1045	TFD	489	MEX	368B	WAL	338	WFD	634	BRN	547	MEX
1046	WFD	490	MEX	370B	SHF	339	NEA	635	STV	548	GOR
1047	WFD	491	MEX	371B	LIV	340	LNG	636	STV	744	MEX
1048	WFD	492	MEX	372B	NEA	341	NEA	637	STV	745	NEA
1049	WFD	493	TFD	374B	WAL	342	NEA	638	SHF	746	MEX

No.	Depot
747	BRN
748	BRN
749	BRN
750	MEX
751	CHR
752	BRN
753	MEX
754	BRN
755	MEX
756	CHR
757	MEX
758	BRN
759	MEX
760	BRN
761	BRN
762	MEX
763	BRN
764	ANN
765	ANN
766	BRN
767	ANN
768	TFD
769	MEX
770	ANN
771	WFD
772	NEA
773	NEA
774	ANN
775	ANN
894	NEA
895	LIV
896	GOR
897	NEA
898	WRX
899	WRX
900	GOR
901	WRX
902	WRX
903	WRX
904	LIV
905	GOR
906	WRX
907	STP
908	WAL
909	STP
910	STP
911	LIV
912	STP
913	NEA
914	CHR
915	STP
916	WRX
917	NEA
918	WAL
919	TFD
920	WRX
921	WAL
922	LIV
923	LEI
924	LIV
925	LIV
926	LEI
927	ANN
928	WRX
929	WRX
930	ANN
931	STP
932	GOR
933	CHR
934	NEA
935	WRX
936	WAL
937	ANN
938	WRX
939	ANN
940	GOR
941	WAL
942	NEA
943	GOR
944	CHR
945	NEA
946	GOR

N6 (18)

No.	Depot
40	LNG
41	TUX
42	LNG
43	LNG
66	TUX
1145B	LNG
1146B	TUX
1147B	LNG
1154	LNG
1155	LNG
1156	LNG
1157	TUX
1158	TUX
1159	LNG
1160	TUX
1161	TUX
1162	LNG
1163	TUX

O4 (131)

No.	Depot
1	GOR
5	GOR
8	GOR
26	GOR
69	MEX
93	GOR
102	GOR
133	MEX
155	GOR
271	ANN
331	MEX
332	MEX
333	MEX
334	GOR
335	MEX
346	MEX
347	MEX
348	MEX
349	MEX
350	MEX
351	ANN
352	GOR
353	GOR
354	GOR
355	GOR
375	ANN
376	MEX
377	GOR
378	GOR
379	GOR
380	ANN
381	SHF
382	SHF
383	SHF
384	MEX
385	SHF
386	MEX
387	ANN
388	MEX
389	ANN
390	MEX
391	MEX
392	MEX
393	GOR
394	GOR
395	GOR
396	GOR
397	MEX
398	MEX
399	SHF
400	MEX
402	MEX
403	IMM
404	MEX
405	MEX
406	MEX
407	MEX
408	ANN
412	GOR
413	GOR
966	GOR
1183	GOR
1184	MEX
1185	MEX
1186	MEX
1187	MEX
1188	MEX
1189	MEX
1190	MEX
1191	MEX
1192	MEX
1193	MEX
1194	MEX
1195	MEX
1196	MEX
1197	MEX
1198	MEX
1199	MEX
1200	MEX
1201	MEX
1202	MEX
1203	IMM
1204	IMM
1205	SHF
1206	KDY
1207	MEX
1208	MEX
1209	MEX
1210	MEX
1211	STV
1212	ANN
1213	ANN
1214	ANN
1215	ANN
1216	ANN
1217	ANN
1218	ANN
1219	ANN
1220	ANN
1221	ANN
1222	MEX
1223	ANN
1224	ANN
1225	ANN
1226	ANN
1227	ANN
1228	ANN
1229	STV
1230	STV
1231	STV
1232	STV
1233	STV
1234	GOR
1235	STV
1236	STV
1237	IMM
1238	ANN
1239	GOR
1240	KDY
1241	MEX
1242	IMM
1243	IMM
1244	IMM
1245	IMM
1246	SHF
1247	SHF
1248	IMM
1249	IMM
1250	IMM
1251	STV
1252	IMM

O5 (17)

No.	Depot
10	MEX
11	MEX
12	MEX
13	MEX
14	SHF
15	SHF
17	SHF
19	SHF
22	SHF
414	RET
415	RET
417	MEX
418	RET
419	RET
420	GOR
421	MEX
422	GOR

Q4 (89)

No.	Depot
39	KDY
44	MEX
48	MEX
49	MEX
56	BRN
57	KDY
58	MEX
59	BRN
62	MEX
63	KDY
64	MEX
65	MEX
67	MEX
68	BRN
70	SHF
71	STV
85	KDY
86	STV
87	BRN
91	BRN
92	GOR
135	MEX
136	MEX
137	BRN
138	STV
139	KDY
140	KDY
142	BRN
143	KDY
144	IMM
145	MEX
146	MEX
147	KDY
148	MEX
149	MEX
150	KDY
151	MEX
152	MEX
153	KDY
159	MEX
160	KDY
161	STV
162	KDY
163	MEX
164	MEX
212	STV
213	SHF
356	MEX
401	MEX
956	KDY
957	LNG
958	MEX
959	LNG
960	MEX
961	MEX
962	MEX
963	MEX
964	IMM
965	MEX
1052	GOR
1053	MEX
1054	MEX
1073	MEX
1074	KDY
1075	MEX
1076	KDY
1077	LNG
1132	LNG
1133	LNG
1134	GOR
1135	LNG
1136	LNG
1137	LNG
1138	LNG
1139	LNG
1140	LNG
1141	LNG
1142	LNG
1143	LNG
1144	KDY
1174	MEX
1175	MEX
1176	LNG
1177	MEX
1178	KDY
1179	LNG
1180	MEX
1181	IMM
1182	MEX

S1 (4)

No.	Depot
1170	MEX
1171	MEX
1172	MEX
1173	MEX

WMCQ (1)

No.	Depot
400B	WRX

X4 (6)

No.	Depot
967	TFD
968	LIV
969	TFD
970	LIV
971	TFD
972	LIV

Y2 (2)

No.	Depot
62B	IMM
63B	IMM

GER 1336

B12 (70)

No.	Shed	No.	Shed	No.	Shed	No.	Shed	No.	Shed	No.	Shed
1500	IPS	1561	IPS	1031	CAM	1820	IPS	408	STR	472	NOR
1501	IPS	1562	IPS	1032	DON	1821	IPS	409	STR	473	COL
1502	IPS	1563	IPS	1033	STR	1822	IPS	410	STR	474	IPS
1503	IPS	1564	IPS	1035	CAM	1823	CAM	411	STR	475	NOR
1504	CAM	1565	IPS	1036	CAM	1824	MAR	412	STR	476	KLN
1505	IPS	1566	IPS	1037	NOR	1825	NOR	413	IPS	477	KLN
1507	CAM	1567	NOR	1039	LIN	1826	NOR	414	STR	478	KLN
1508	PKS	1568	NOR			1827	NOR	415	STR	479	CAM
1509	NOR	1569	NOR	**D14** (21)		1828	STR	416	STR	480	KLN
1510	NOR	1570	NOR			1829	STR	417	CAM	481	IPS
1511	PKS			1862	STR	1830	MAR	418	KLN	482	KLN
1512	CAM	**D13** (58)		1864	STR	1831	NOR	419	KLN	483	DON
1513	NOR			1865	STR	1832	IPS	420	NOR	484	MAR
1514	CAM	700	DON	1866	STR	1833	CAM	421	IPS	485	NOR
1515	IPS	704	PBE	1867	COL	1834	STR	422	IPS	486	NOR
1516	NOR	705	PBE	1868	IPS	1835	MAR	423	NOR	487	NOR
1517	NOR	706	MAR	1870	IPS	1836	NOR	424	KLN	488	YAR
1518	IPS	707	NOR	1871	COL	1837	YAR	425	IPS	489	YAR
1519	IPS	708	CAM	1872	STR	1838	STR	426	NOR	490	NOR
1520	CAM	710	PBE	1873	IPS	1839	PKS	427	STR	491	NOR
1521	CAM	712	CAM	1875	STR	1840	CAM	428	NOR	492	NOR
1522	CAM	713	PBE	1876	CAM	1841	IPS	429	NOR	493	LOW
1523	IPS	717	MAR	1877	NOR	1842	IPS	430	CAM	494	NOR
1524	CAM	718	KLN	1878	NOR	1843	YAR	431	STR	495	NOR
1525	STR	719	PBE	1879	NOR	1844	PKS	432	CAM	496	NOR
1526	CAM	728	CAM	1881	LOW	1845	NOR	433	CAM	497	YAR
1527	CAM	729	MAR	1886	STR	1846	COL	434	PBE	498	IPS
1528	CAM	730	YAR	1892	CAM	1847	STR	435	PBE	499	PBE
1529	IPS	731	IPS	1893	CAM	1848	STR	436	CAM	500	CAM
1530	CAM	732	PBE	1895	MAR	1849	STR	437	KLN	501	CAM
1531	STR	733	COL	1900	STR	1850	STR	438	CAM	502	CAM
1532	PKS	734	COL			1851	STR	439	NOR	503	KLN
1533	STR	735	PKS	**D15** (90)		1852	STR	440	NOR	504	CAM
1534	STR	737	IPS			1853	STR	441	MAR	505	MAR
1535	IPS	738	IPS	1790	CAM	1854	STR	442	NOR	506	MAR
1536	PKS	739	COL	1791	STR	1855	COL	443	NOR		
1537	IPS	741	IPS	1792	CAM	1856	STR	444	KLN	**F3** (50)	
1538	IPS	742	CAM	1793	STR	1857	STR	445	NOR		
1539	IPS	744	COL	1794	KLN	1858	IPS	446	NOR	1040	STR
1540	IPS	745	COL	1795	STR	1859	IPS	447	NOR	1041	STR
1541	STR	748	COL	1796	STR	1860	STR	448	NOR	1042	PKS
1542	STR	751	MAR	1797	CAM	1861	STR	449	LOW	1043	STR
1543	STR	756	COL	1798	STR	1863	NOR	450	NOR	1044	KLN
1544	STR	765	IPS	1799	STR	1869	IPS	451	NOR	1045	NOR
1545	STR	766	NOR	1800	YAR	1874	IPS	452	NOR	1046	COL
1546	STR	767	NOR	1801	YAR	1880	YAR	453	LOW	1047	NOR
1547	STR	772	PBE	1802	CAM	1882	IPS	454	CAM	1048	NOR
1548	STR	775	PBE	1803	IPS	1883	NOR	455	CAM	1049	NOR
1549	STR	777	MAR	1804	STR	1884	NOR	456	CAM	1060	STR
1550	STR	779	CAM	1805	STR	1885	NOR	457	CAM	1061	CAM
1551	STR	1012	CAM	1806	IPS	1887	NOR	458	KLN	1062	STR
1552	IPS	1013	YAR	1807	IPS	1888	IPS	459	CAM	1063	CAM
1553	STR	1015	CAM	1808	CAM	1889	CAM	460	CAM	1064	IPS
1554	STR	1016	CAM	1809	NOR	1890	CAM	461	STR	1065	IPS
1555	STR	1018	KLN	1810	MAR	1891	CAM	462	KLN	1066	IPS
1556	STR	1020	DON	1811	CAM	1894	CAM	463	CAM	1067	COL
1557	STR	1021	CAM	1812	CAM	1896	KLN	464	KLN	1068	IPS
1558	STR	1023	CAM	1813	COL	1897	COL	465	IPS	1069	COL
1559	STR	1025	LIN	1814	CAM	1898	PKS	466	IPS	1070	IPS
1560	STR	1026	STR	1815	IPS	1899	DON	467	IPS	1071	IPS
		1027	STR	1816	CAM			468	IPS	1072	IPS
		1028	LIN	1817	STR	**E4** (100)		469	IPS	1073	IPS
		1029	MAR	1818	STR			470	IPS	1074	PKS
		1030	PBE	1819	STR	407	STR	471	IPS	1075	PKS

N7 No.1011, the last locomotive built by the Great Eastern before Grouping, stands at Stratford shed wearing its number and little else to signify ownership.

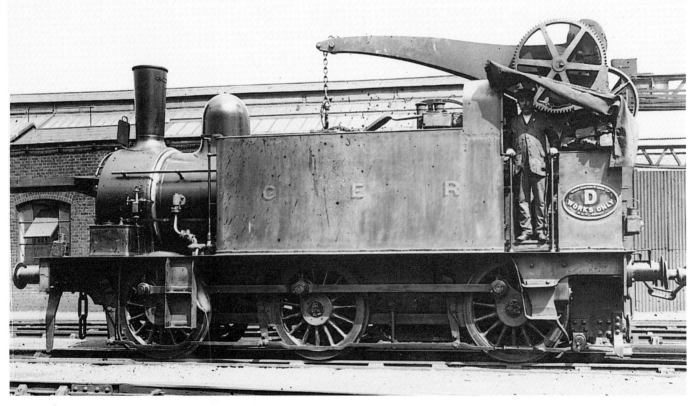

At Stratford works were three 0-6-0 crane tanks included in their Departmental Stock. From October 1894, the numbers 204/5/6, carried hitherto, were changed to letters B, C, and D, prominently displayed on large brass plates.

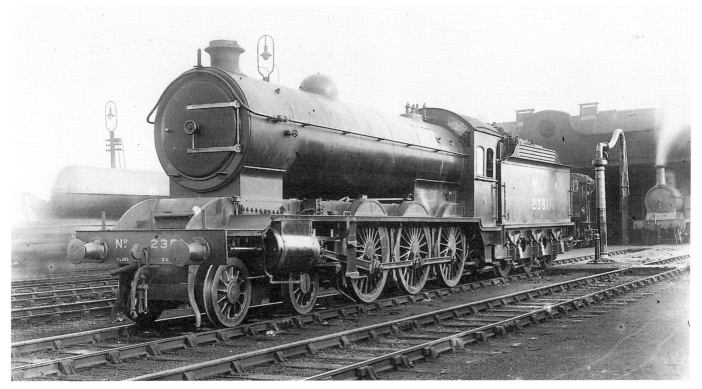

Although not built on FIRST DAY, B16 No.2381 shows the former North Eastern classification S3 on its bufferbeam whilst LNER adorns its tender. The engine was photographed at the ex-GC shed at Neasden 18th June 1924 after working in from York.

Gorton based B3 No.1165 VALOUR, resplendent in Great Central livery, is made ready for its return working at Leicester shed after bringing in a Manchester - Marylebone express. The date is 9th June 1923.

No.	Code
1076	COL
1077	IPS
1078	NOR
1079	NOR
1080	STR
1081	STR
1082	KLN
1083	STR
1084	KLN
1085	CAM
1086	NOR
1087	NOR
1088	NOR
1089	LOW
1090	YAR
1091	NOR
1092	NOR
1093	NOR
1094	LOW
1095	LOW
1096	LOW
1097	LOW
1098	LOW
1099	NOR

F4 (118)

No.	Code
71	STR
72	STR
73	STR
74	STR
75	STR
76	STR
77	STR
78	STR
79	STR
80	STR
92	STR
93	STR
97	STR
98	STR
99	STR
101	STR
102	STR
105	STR
106	STR
107	STR
111	STR
140	STR
146	COL
148	PKS
149	COL
171	STR
172	STR
173	STR
174	STR
175	STR
176	STR
177	STR
178	STR
180	STR
181	STR
182	STR
183	STR
184	STR
185	STR
186	STR
187	STR
189	STR
211	STR
212	STR
213	STR
214	STR
215	STR
216	STR
217	STR
218	STR
219	STR
220	STR
221	STR
222	STR
223	STR
224	STR
225	STR
232	STR
233	STR
234	STR
235	STR
236	STR
237	STR
238	STR
239	STR
240	STR
241	STR
242	STR
243	STR
244	STR
572	STR
573	STR
574	STR
575	STR
576	STR
577	STR
578	STR
579	STR
580	STR
581	STR
582	STR
583	STR
584	STR
585	STR
586	STR
587	STR
588	STR
591	STR
650	STR
653	STR
654	LOW
655	STR
657	STR
659	STR
660	STR
662	STR
663	STR
665	IPS
666	NOR
668	STR
669	STR
670	STR
674	STR
675	STR
676	STR
677	NOR
678	LOW
679	STR
791	STR
792	STR
793	STR
794	STR
795	STR
796	STR
797	STR
798	STR
799	CAM
800	STR

F5 (30)

No.	Code
91	STR
94	STR
95	STR
96	STR
100	STR
103	STR
104	STR
108	STR
109	STR
110	STR
141	COL
142	STR
143	STR
144	IPS
145	STR
147	IPS
170	STR
179	STR
188	STR
589	STR
590	STR
780	STR
781	STR
782	STR
783	STR
784	STR
785	STR
786	STR
787	STR
788	STR

F6 (22)

No.	Code
1	STR
2	STR
3	STR
4	STR
5	STR
6	STR
7	STR
8	STR
9	STR
10	STR
61	STR
62	STR
63	STR
64	STR
65	STR
66	STR
67	STR
68	STR
69	STR
70	STR
789	STR
790	STR

F7 (12)

No.	Code
1300	COL
1301	COL
1302	CAM
1303	STR
1304	STR
1305	STR
1306	STR
1307	CAM
1308	CAM
1309	STR
1310	CAM
1311	STR

G4 (40)

No.	Code
1100	STR
1101	STR
1102	STR
1103	STR
1104	STR
1105	STR
1106	STR
1107	STR
1108	STR
1109	STR
1110	STR
1111	STR
1112	STR
1113	STR
1114	STR
1115	STR
1116	STR
1117	STR
1118	STR
1119	STR
1120	STR
1121	STR
1122	STR
1123	STR
1124	STR
1125	STR
1126	STR
1127	STR
1128	STR
1129	STR
1130	STR
1131	STR
1132	STR
1133	STR
1134	STR
1135	STR
1136	STR
1137	STR
1138	STR
1139	STR

J14 (18)

No.	Code
604	STR
951	COL
959	COL
963	PBE
964	YAR
970	KLN
973	KLN
976	COL
977	COL
978	COL
980	STR
981	STR
983	PKS
984	IPS
985	STR
987	STR
993	MAR
998	NOR

J15 (272)

No.	Code
37	IPS
38	IPS
39	IPS
119	LOW
120	NOR
121	LOW
122	LOW
124	LOW
507	STR
508	CAM
509	CAM
510	CAM
511	CAM
512	MAR
514	STR
515	STR
516	STR
517	STR
518	MAR
519	STR
520	CAM
521	MAR
522	MAR
523	LIN
524	MAR
525	IPS
526	CAM
527	CAM
528	LIN
529	CAM
530	CAM
531	CAM
532	CAM
533	MAR
534	STR
535	CAM
536	CAM
537	IPS
538	IPS
539	COL
540	COL
541	COL
542	YAR
543	NOR
544	NOR
545	IPS
546	IPS
547	PBE
548	CAM
549	CAM
550	STR
551	STR
552	STR
553	STR
554	STR
555	CAM
556	STR
557	STR
558	STR
559	IPS
560	STR
561	STR
562	NOR
563	CAM
564	NOR
565	NOR
566	IPS
567	COL
568	IPS
569	IPS
570	CAM
571	CAM
592	IPS
593	IPS
594	IPS
595	IPS
596	IPS
597	IPS
598	IPS
599	IPS
600	COL
609	NOR
610	NOR
611	NOR
612	NOR
613	LOW
614	NOR
615	NOR
616	NOR
617	NOR
618	LIN
620	NOR
621	PBE
622	STR
623	STR
625	KLN
627	MAR
628	MAR
629	NOR

No.		No.		No.		No.		No.		No.	
630	NOR	833	CAM	900	STR	1168	NOR	1227	MAR	1277	MAR
631	LOW	834	CAM	901	STR	1171	CAM	1228	MAR	1278	MAR
633	NOR	835	CAM	902	STR	1172	CAM	1229	MAR	1279	MAR
634	NOR	836	CAM	903	STR	1175	CAM	1230	MAR	1280	MAR
635	YAR	837	CAM	904	STR	1176	CAM	1231	LIN	1281	MAR
636	YAR	838	CAM	905	STR	1177	CAM	1232	MAR	1282	CAM
638	NOR	839	CAM	906	STR	1178	CAM	1233	LIN	1283	CAM
639	NOR	840	CAM	907	STR	1179	CAM	1234	MAR	1284	CAM
640	STR	841	KLN	908	CAM	1180	CAM	1235	STR	1285	MAR
641	IPS	842	CAM	909	STR	1181	CAM	1236	CAM	1286	CAM
642	COL	843	CAM	910	STR	1182	CAM	1237	MAR	1287	CAM
643	STR	844	STR	911	STR	1183	CAM	1238	MAR	1288	CAM
644	STR	845	CAM	912	STR	1184	MAR	1239	MAR	1289	MAR
645	STR	846	MAR	913	STR	1185	MAR			1290	MAR
646	CAM	847	KLN	914	IPS	1186	MAR	**J18** (10)		1291	MAR
647	STR	848	CAM	915	STR	1187	LIN			1292	MAR
648	STR	849	CAM	916	STR	1188	MAR	1240	STR	1293	MAR
649	STR	850	STR	917	STR	1190	CAM	1241	MAR	1294	CAM
680	MAR	851	CAM	918	STR	1191	CAM	1242	MAR		
681	MAR	852	STR	919	PBE	1192	MAR	1243	MAR	**J65** (20)	
682	MAR	853	STR	920	CAM	1195	MAR	1244	MAR		
683	MAR	854	PBE	921	CAM	1196	MAR	1245	CAM	150	PKS
684	PBE	855	STR	922	STR	1199	CAM	1246	CAM	151	CAM
685	MAR	856	CAM	923	STR	1200	PBE	1247	MAR	152	CAM
686	PBE	857	CAM	924	COL	1203	PBE	1248	MAR	153	STR
688	PBE	858	PBE	925	COL	1204	PBE	1249	MAR	154	NOR
689	MAR	859	PBE	926	COL	1205	PBE			155	STR
690	COL	860	STR	927	COL	1206	PBE	**J19** (25)		156	STR
691	COL	861	STR	928	CAM	1208	PBE			157	STR
692	COL	862	STR	929	CAM	1209	PBE	1140	PBE	158	STR
693	COL	863	STR	930	PBE			1141	PBE	159	LOW
694	IPS	864	STR	931	PBE	**J17** (44)		1142	PBE	245	IPS
696	STR	865	STR	932	STR			1143	PBE	246	IPS
697	STR	866	NOR	933	IPS	1153	PBE	1144	PBE	247	IPS
698	STR	867	STR	934	IPS	1156	PBE	1145	PBE	248	PKS
699	STR	868	STR	936	IPS	1169	PBE	1146	PBE	249	STR
801	KLN	869	STR	937	IPS	1170	PBE	1147	PBE	250	PKS
802	KLN	870	STR	938	STR	1173	CAM	1148	PBE	251	PKS
803	MAR	871	STR	939	IPS	1174	CAM	1149	PBE	252	IPS
805	CAM	872	STR	940	IPS	1189	CAM	1250	MAR	253	PKS
806	CAM	873	STR	941	IPS	1193	CAM	1251	CAM	254	IPS
807	NOR	874	STR	942	IPS	1194	MAR	1252	CAM		
809	NOR	875	STR	943	IPS	1197	MAR	1253	MAR	**J66** (49+1)	
810	NOR	876	STR	944	PKS	1198	CAM	1254	CAM		
812	LOW	877	STR	945	PKS	1201	PBE	1260	MAR	275	MAR
813	NOR	878	STR			1202	PBE	1261	MAR	276	MAR
814	YAR	879	STR	**J16** (46)		1207	PBE	1262	MAR	277	MAR
815	NOR	880	STR			1210	NOR	1263	MAR	278	MAR
816	NOR	881	STR	1150	PBE	1211	PBE	1264	MAR	279	MAR
817	NOR	883	STR	1151	PBE	1212	PBE	1265	CAM	280	MAR
818	NOR	886	STR	1152	PBE	1213	PBE	1266	MAR	281	STR W
819	NOR	887	STR	1154	PBE	1214	PBE	1267	CAM	282	LIN
820	NOR	888	STR	1155	PBE	1215	PBE	1268	CAM	283	MAR
821	PBE	889	STR	1157	PBE	1216	PBE	1269	CAM	284	MAR
823	STR	890	MAR	1158	PBE	1217	PBE			285	PBE
824	NOR	891	STR	1159	PBE	1218	PBE	**J20** (25)		286	STR
825	CAM	892	STR	1160	PBE	1219	PBE			287	KLN
826	CAM	893	STR	1161	PBE	1220	PBE	1270	CAM	288	STR
827	PBE	894	STR	1162	PBE	1221	PBE	1271	MAR	289	MAR
828	NOR	895	STR	1163	PBE	1222	PBE	1272	CAM	290	KLN
829	NOR	896	STR	1164	PBE	1223	MAR	1273	CAM	291	CAM
830	NOR	897	CAM	1165	PBE	1224	MAR	1274	CAM	292	IPS
831	CAM	898	STR	1166	PBE	1225	MAR	1275	MAR	293	COL
832	CAM	899	STR	1167	PBE	1226	MAR	1276	MAR	294	STR

295	IPS		263	STR		89	STR		370	STR		**Y4** (4+1)				**_GNR_ 1359**	
296	IPS		264	STR		90	STR		371	STR							
297	IPS		327	COL		160	YAR		372	STR		210	STR W			**A1** (2)	
298	CAM		329	STR		162	CAM		373	STR		226	STR				
299	LIN		330	CAM		163	NOR		374	STR		227	STR			1470	DON
300	LIN		331	STR		165	STR		375	STR		228	STR			1471	DON
301	KLN		332	STR		166	STR		376	STR		229	STR				
302	STR		333	IPS		167	NOR		377	STR						**C1** (94)	
303	STR		334	COL		168	STR		378	STR		**Y5** (2+2)					
304	STR		336	IPS		190	NOR		379	STR						251	DON
307	CAM		397	CAM		191	PBE		380	STR		209	LOW			272	DON
308	KLN		398	KLN		192	STR		381	STR		0228	STR W			273	DON
309	KLN		399	CAM		193	STR		382	STR		230	STR W			274	KX
310	STR		400	PBE		194	STR		383	STR		231	COL			275	GRA
311	STR		401	PBE		195	STR		384	IPS						276	DON
312	STR		402	KLN		196	STR		385	STR		**Y6** (6)				277	KX
313	PBE		403	KLN		197	STR		386	STR						278	KX
314	NOR		404	CAM		198	CAM		387	STR		0125	WIS			279	KX
315	IPS		405	CAM		265	STR		388	STR		0126	WIS			280	DON
316	STR		406	MAR		266	STR		389	STR		0129	WIS			281	GRA
317	NOR					267	STR		390	STR		132	WIS			282	GRA
318	CAM		**J68** (20)			268	STR		391	STR		133	WIS			283	GRA
319	MAR					269	STR		392	STR		134	WIS			284	GRA
320	NOR		21	STR		270	STR		393	STR						285	GRA
321	PBE		22	STR		271	STR		394	STR						286	GRA
322	IPS		23	STR		272	STR		395	STR						287	GRA
323	IPS		24	STR		273	CAM		396	STR						288	NWE
324	STR		25	STR		274	STR									289	NWE
325	NOR		26	STR		305	STR		**J70** (12)							290	NWE
326	LOW		27	CAM		328	MAR									291	NWE
			28	MAR		335	IPS		125	IPS						292	NWE
J67 (51)			29	PBE		337	STR		126	IPS						293	GRA
			30	PBE		338	STR		127	IPS						294	GRA
11	CAM		41	STR		339	STR		128	YAR						295	DON
12	CAM		42	STR		340	STR		129	IPS						296	GRA
13	IPS		43	STR		341	STR		130	IPS						297	GRA
14	STR		44	STR		342	STR		131	CAM						298	DON
15	STR		45	STR		343	STR		135	IPS						299	KX
16	IPS		46	STR		344	STR		136	WIS						300	DON
17	STR		47	STR		345	STR		137	YAR						301	KX
18	STR		48	STR		346	STR		138	YAR						1300	NWE
19	STR		49	STR		347	STR		139	IPS						1400	KX
20	STR		50	STR		348	STR									1401	GRA
161	NOR					349	STR		**J92** (3)							1402	GRA
164	NOR		**J69** (109)			350	STR									1403	GRA
169	KLN					351	STR		B	STR W						1404	GRA
199	CAM		51	STR		352	STR		C	STR W						1405	GRA
200	STR		52	STR		353	STR		D	STR W						1406	GRA
201	STR		53	STR		354	STR									1407	NWE
202	STR		54	STR		355	STR		**N7** (12)							1408	NWE
203	STR		55	IPS		356	STR									1409	NWE
204	STR		56	STR		357	STR		1000	STR						1410	NWE
205	STR		57	STR		358	STR		1001	STR						1411	CAM
206	STR		58	STR		359	STR		1002	STR						1412	NWE
207	STR		59	STR		360	STR		1003	STR						1413	NWE
208	STR		60	STR		361	STR		1004	STR						1414	GRA
255	STR		81	STR		362	CAM		1005	STR						1415	GRA
256	STR		82	STR		363	STR		1006	STR						1416	GRA
257	STR		83	STR		364	COL		1007	STR						1417	GRA
258	STR		84	STR		365	STR		1008	STR						1418	GRA
259	STR		85	STR		366	STR		1009	STR						1419	DON
260	STR		86	STR		367	STR		1010	STR						1420	DON
261	STR		87	STR		368	STR		1011	STR						1421	NWE
262	STR		88	STR		369	STR									1422	DON

No.	Shed
1423	DON
1424	DON
1425	DON
1426	CAM
1427	KX
1428	KX
1429	NWE
1430	GRA
1431	GRA
1432	GRA
1433	GRA
1434	DON
1435	DON
1436	DON
1437	NWE
1438	NWE
1439	NWE
1440	KX
1441	KX
1442	KX
1443	KX
1444	KX
1445	NWE
1446	GRA
1447	GRA
1448	DON
1449	DON
1450	KX
1451	DON
1452	DON
1453	DON
1454	DON
1455	DON
1456	DON
1457	GRA
1458	KX
1459	KX
1460	KX
1461	KX

C2 (22)

No.	Shed
250	DON
252	CAM
253	CAM
254	CAM
255	NWE
256	NWE
257	NWE
258	NWE
259	NWE
260	DON
271	DON
949	CAM
950	YK
982	NWE
983	YK
984	YK
985	NWE
986	DON
987	NWE
988	NWE
989	NWE
990	NWE

C12 (60)

No.	Shed
1009A	BFD
1010	COP
1013	BFD
1014	COP
1015	BFD
1016	LIN
1017	BFD
1018	BFD
1019	ARD
1020	BFD
1501	COP
1502	HAT
1503	LTH
1504	BOS
1505	NWE
1506	LTH
1507	NWE
1508	NWE
1509	BOS
1510	BOS
1511	CLK
1512	HAT
1513	LTH
1514	HAT
1515	CLK
1516	NWE
1517	CLK
1518	BOS
1519	CLK
1520	CLK
1521	NWE
1522	NWE
1523	CLK
1524	CLK
1525	GRA
1526	CLK
1527	GRA
1528	ARD
1529	GRA
1530	CLK
1531	COP
1532	COP
1533	GRA
1534	HAT
1535	COP
1536	BFD
1537	HAT
1538	COP
1539	ARD
1540	BFD
1541	HAT
1542	ARD
1543	BFD
1544	BFD
1545	BFD
1546	BFD
1547	BFD
1548	HAT
1549	BFD
1550	HAT

D1 (15)

No.	Shed
51	COP
52	COP
53	COP
54	COP
55	COP
56	CAM
57	GRA
58	GRA
59	GRA
60	CAM
61	CAM
62	CAM
63	NWE
64	NWE
65	NWE

D2 (70)

No.	Shed
41	KX
42	KX
43	COP
44	COP
45	BOS
46	LIN
47	YK
48	YK
49	HIT
50	HIT
1180	YK
1321	KX
1322	KX
1323	YK
1324	RET
1325	DON
1326	COP
1327	CLK
1328	DON
1329	CLK
1330	YK
1331	YK
1332	GRA
1333	KX
1334	DON
1335	DON
1336	HIT
1337	HIT
1338	GRA
1339	GRA
1340	KX
1361	CLK
1362	DON
1363	CLK
1364	CLK
1365	LEI
1366	KX
1367	BOS
1368	LIN
1369	LIN
1370	RET
1371	BOS
1372	YK
1373	CLK
1374	GRA
1375	CLK
1376	COP
1377	HAT
1378	DON
1379	BOS
1380	BOS
1381	RET
1382	BOS
1383	LTH
1384	BOS
1385	HIT
1386	DON
1387	DON
1388	HIT
1389	HIT
1390	YK
1391	KX
1392	LIN
1393	CLK
1394	BOS
1395	BOS
1396	DON
1397	DON
1398	DON
1399	CLK

D3 (45)

No.	Shed
400	CLK
1071	YK
1072	HIT
1073	HIT
1074	RET
1075	COP
1076	COP
1078	HAT
1080	HIT
1301	BFD
1302	ARD
1303	LIN
1304	LTH
1305	CLK
1306	CLK
1307	LTH
1308	YK
1309	CLK
1310	CLK
1311	BFD
1312	KX
1314	KX
1315	CLK
1316	CLK
1317	CLK
1318	CLK
1319	LEI
1320	CLK
1341	DON
1342	DON
1343	BOS
1344	RET
1345	DON
1346	KX
1347	DON
1348	DON
1349	DON
1350	BOS
1351	YK
1352	LEI
1353	CLK
1354	CLK
1355	CLK
1357	BOS
1359	BOS

D4 (6)

No.	Shed
1077	GRA
1079	GRA
1313	LIN
1356	BOS
1358	BOS
1360	BOS

E1 (34)

No.	Shed
715	GRA
753	BOS
755	BOS
758	BOS
760	CLK
812	GRA
814	LTH
818	CLK
861	GRA
864	CLK
867	LIN
868	GRA
882	GRA
883	LIN
884	GRA
885	BOS
887	LIN
893	GRA
897	CLK
992	CLK
993	RET
994	BOS
995	BOS
998	BOS
999	BOS
1000A	LTH
1061	BOS
1062	LIN
1063	LIN
1064	BOS
1067	LIN
1068	BOS
1069	LIN
1070	RET

G1 (12)

No.	Shed
766	BFD
767	HAT
769	CLK
770	HAT
824	CLK
827	BFD
828	CLK
830	CLK
932	BFD
939	NWE
940	CLK
943	BOS

G2 (6)

No.	Shed
659	COP
682	BFD
694	COP
695	BFD
696	COP
765	NWE

J1 (15)

No.	Shed
1	HAT
2	HAT
3	HAT
4	CLK
5	BFD
6	BFD
7	HIT
8	BFD
9	BFD
10	HIT
11	HAT
12	KX
13	BOS
14	BOS
15	BOS

J2 (10)

No.	Shed
71	BFD
72	NWE
73	BOS
74	NWE
75	NWE
76	CLK
77	CLK
78	CLK
79	DON
80	BFD

J3 (69)

No.	Shed
177	CLK
303	CLK
306	CLK
308	CLK
316	CLK
342	HIT
343	CLK
344	DON
350	RET
351	DON
362	DON
375	LEI
379	CLK
381	DON

384	HAT	170A	BFD	725	DON	1112	CLK	534	NWE	598	DON
386	DON	175A	ARD	726	DON	1116	CLK	535	DON	599	BOS
387	HIT	179	CLK	727	NWE	1117	CLK	536	TFD	600	BOS
388	ARD	180	DON	729	ARD	1118	DON	537	TFD	601	CLK
390	NWE	181	NWE	730	LIN	1121	RET	538	TFD	602	BOS
399	ARD	182	COP	731	LIN	1122	BFD	539	HIT	603	NWE
717	KX	187	ARD	734	ARD	1125	DON	540	CLK	604	BOS
1045	DON	191	BOS	744	ARD	1129	DON	541	CLK	605	NWE
1082	NWE	192	DON	745	KX	1131	DON	542	CLK	606	DON
1091	CLK	193	NWE	746	DON	1135	DON	543	CLK	607	DON
1094	CLK	195	BOS	748	DON	1138	HSY	544	CLK	608	DON
1096	CLK	196	RET	750	BFD	1140	COP	545	CLK	609	DON
1099	HIT	198	NWE	792	RET	1143	CLK	546	DON	610	DON
1100	HAT	199	CLK	793	RET	1144	CLK	547	ARD	621	NWE
1103	NWE	302	KX	797	BFD	1145	BOS	548	NWE	622	NWE
1104	NWE	304	GRA	799	ARD	1149	DON	549	CLK	623	NWE
1105	NWE	307	ARD	831	RET	1150	BFD	550	CLK	624	NWE
1108	NWE	312	NWE	832	BOS	1153	BFD	551	CLK	625	NWE
1109	LIN	313	HIT	833	DON	1154	DON	552	CLK	626	CLK
1113	CLK	314	HIT	834	KX	1155	DON	553	TFD	627	CLK
1114	GRA	315	DON	837	RET	1158	DON	554	NWE	628	CLK
1115	CLK	317	LIN	838	DON	1160	DON	555	NWE	629	CLK
1119	CLK	318	CLK	839	DON	1166	CLK	556	DON	630	CLK
1120	CLK	323	ARD	840	COP	1171	ARD	557	CLK	631	DON
1123	DON	329	CLK	843	COP	1172	COP	558	CLK	632	DON
1124	DON	331	ARD	844	HSY			559	ARD	633	BOS
1126	DON	332	GRA	845	BOS	**J5** (20)		560	ARD	634	BOS
1127	DON	334	CLK	846	DON			561	CLK	635	DON
1128	DON	336	ARD	848	BFD	21	DON	562	CLK	636	DON
1130	RET	337	RET	849	CLK	22	RET	563	CLK	637	DON
1132	DON	338	RET	850	ARD	23	RET	564	CLK	638	DON
1133	DON	339	NWE	1011	COP	24	RET	565	CLK	639	DON
1134	DON	345	DON	1012	ARD	25	DON	566	CLK		
1136	HSY	348	CLK	1031	CLK	26	DON	567	DON	**J7** (10)	
1137	HIT	349	ARD	1032	BOS	27	CLK	568	TFD		
1139	HIT	352	CLK	1033	CLK	28	LEI	569	TFD	156A	CLK
1141	CLK	353	DON	1034	CLK	29	DON	570	DON	188	CLK
1142	CLK	354	ARD	1035	CLK	30	CLK	571	BOS	374	ARD
1146	BFD	359	RET	1036	HSY	31	RET	572	BOS	1021	CLK
1147	BFD	361	CLK	1037	HIT	32	RET	573	CLK	1023	CLK
1151	CLK	365	BFD	1039	LIN	33	CLK	574	CLK	1024	CLK
1152	COP	368	DON	1040	CLK	34	RET	575	CLK	1027	ARD
1156	DON	371	ARD	1041	CLK	35	DON	576	CLK	1028	ARD
1157	DON	372	BFD	1043	COP	36	RET	577	CLK	1029	ARD
1159	DON	373	KX	1044	ARD	37	DON	578	NWE	1030	BFD
1161	CLK	378	ARD	1081	LIN	38	GRA	579	NWE		
1162	CLK	383	HSY	1083	BOS	39	GRA	580	CLK	**J50** (10)	
1163	CLK	385	NWE	1084	BFD	40	GRA	581	CLK		
1164	CLK	392	NWE	1085	LIN			582	BOS	221	ARD
1165	CLK	394	LIN	1086	ARD	**J6** (110)		583	CLK	222	ARD
1167	RET	396	CLK	1087	NWE			584	KX	223	ARD
1168	CLK	398	BFD	1088	HIT	521	CLK	585	HIT	224	ARD
1169	HAT	640A	BFD	1090	BFD	522	CLK	586	TFD	225	ARD
1170	HSY	641	HIT	1092	GRA	523	GRA	587	CLK	226	ARD
1173	DON	642	KX	1093	GRA	524	CLK	588	CLK	227	ARD
		643	RET	1095	CLK	525	CLK	589	NWE	228	ARD
J4 (159)		644	LIN	1097	BFD	526	CLK	590	DON	229	ARD
		646	RET	1098	BFD	527	CLK	591	DON	230	ARD
101	HAT	648	RET	1101	ARD	528	CLK	592	KX		
102	BFD	716	HIT	1102	NWE	529	GRA	593	NWE	**J51** (30)	
135A	COP	718	ARD	1106	BOS	530	GRA	594	NWE		
147A	ARD	719	ARD	1107	GRA	531	NWE	595	BOS	157	ARD
150A	BFD	721	CLK	1110	LIN	532	NWE	596	NWE	158	ARD
165	CLK	724	RET	1111	CLK	533	DON	597	NWE	159	BFD

No.	Depot	No.	Depot	No.	Depot	No.	Depot	No.	Depot	No.	Depot
160	ARD	1237	DON	926	HSY	692	BOS	915	COP	1665	NWE
161	ARD	1238	DON	927	HSY	693	TFD	916	BFD	1666	KX
162	BFD	1239	DON	928	ARD	780	DON	917	CLK	1667	KX
163	ARD	1240	KX	929	BFD	781	BOS	918	CLK	1668	KX
164	BFD	1241	DON	930	BFD	784	DON			1669	KX
166	BFD	1242	DON	961	KX	785	KX	**J56** (5)		1670	DON
167	ARD	1243	DON	962	BFD	786	KX			1671	KX
168	ARD	1244A	DON	963	COP	788	BOS	608A	LIN	1672	DON
169	ARD	1245	DON	964	HSY	789	NWE	611	DON	1673	DON
170	BFD	1246	DON	965	CLK	801	DON	612	KX	1674	KX
171	ARD	1247	DON	966	CLK	804	BFD	613	CLK	1675	ARD
172	COP	1248	DON	967	BFD	805	BFD	615	KX	1676	ARD
173	ARD	1249	DON	968	ARD	807	DON			1677	DON
174	BFD	1250	DON	969	HSY	808	BFD	**J57** (8)		1678	DON
175	ARD	1251	HSY	971	HSY	852	DON			1679	KX
176	ARD	1252	HSY	972	HSY	853	BFD	134A	GRA	1680	NWE
178	ARD	1253	KX	973	DON	855	HAT	140A	DON	1681	NWE
211	ARD	1254	HSY	974	HSY	856	BOS	144A	KX	1682	NWE
212	ARD	1255	KX	975	HSY	857	KX	149A	HIT	1683	NWE
213	ARD	1256	HSY	976	HSY	858	COP	684	KX	1684	NWE
214	COP	1257	HSY	978	ARD	859	COP	685	KX	1685	DON
215	ARD	1258	DON	979	HSY	860	COP	686	KX	1686	DON
216	ARD	1259	CLK	980	BFD	901	HAT	687	KX	1687	DON
217	ARD	1260	CLK	1046	HSY	902	COP			1688	DON
218	ARD	1261	KX	1047	HSY	903	BFD	**K1** (8)		1689	DON
219	ARD	1262	KX	1048	HSY	904	BFD			1690	DON
220	ARD	1263	TFD	1049	DON	905	GRA	1630	CLK	1691	DON
		1264	DON	1050	HSY	906	CLK	1632	KX	1692	DON
J52 (88)		1265	TFD	1051	HSY	907	BOS	1633	CLK	1693	DON
		1266	DON	1052	ARD	908	LIN	1634	ARD	1694	DON
970	HSY	1267	NWE	1053	BFD	909	KX	1636	NWE	1695	NWE
977	ARD	1268	NWE	1054	HSY	910	KX	1637	NWE	1696	NWE
1060	HSY	1269	NWE	1055	CLK	911	DON	1638	CLK	1697	NWE
1201	DON	1270	NWE	1056	HSY	912	BFD	1639	CLK	1698	NWE
1202	DON	1271	DON	1057	HSY	914	BFD			1699	NWE
1203	DON	1272	DON	1058	HSY	919	TFD	**K2** (67)		1700	NWE
1204	KX	1273	TFD	1059	HSY	920	CLK			1701	NWE
1205	TFD	1274	TFD	1211	NWE			1631	CLK	1702	NWE
1206	TFD	1275	KX	1212	KX	**J55** (28)		1635	CLK	1703	NWE
1207	ARD	1276	LIN	1213	KX			1640	ARD	1704	NWE
1208	CLK	1277	NWE	1214	KX	397	BFD	1641	NWE		
1209	NWE	1278	NWE	1215	KX	473A	KX	1642	DON	**K3** (10)	
1210	GRA	1279	NWE			496	BFD	1643	NWE		
1216	NWE	1280	NWE	**J54** (56)		610A	LIN	1644	NWE	1000	NWE
1217	LIN	1281	KX			620	BOS	1645	KX	1001	NWE
1218	NWE	1282	KX	139A	KX	636A	BFD	1646	NWE	1002	NWE
1219	NWE	1283	ARD	153A	BOS	638A	LIN	1647	NWE	1003	NWE
1220	NWE	1284	ARD	494	BFD	672	CLK	1648	ARD	1004	DON
1221	NWE	1285	HSY	617	LIN	674	CLK	1649	KX	1005	DON
1222	NWE	1286	DON	619	GRA	677	BFD	1650	DON	1006	DON
1223	NWE	1287	DON	633A	BFD	678	CLK	1651	KX	1007	NWE
1224	NWE	1288	DON	634A	BFD	779	DON	1652	ARD	1008	KX
1225	NWE	1289	NWE	635A	GRA	782	DON	1653	KX	1009	KX
1226	ARD	1290	NWE	637A	DON	783	DON	1654	KX		
1227	HSY			673	CLK	787	DON	1655	KX	**N1** (54)	
1228	HSY	**J53** (49)		675	HIT	790	BOS	1656	KX		
1229	HSY			676	KX	802	BFD	1657	DON	190	HAT
1230	HSY	111	KX	679	ARD	803	DON	1658	ARD	1551	HSY
1231	HSY	155A	DON	680	CLK	806	COP	1659	DON	1552	HSY
1232	HSY	921	HSY	681	BFD	809	BFD	1660	NWE	1553	HSY
1233	HSY	922	HSY	688	DON	810	COP	1661	NWE	1554	BFD
1234	HSY	923	HSY	689	CLK	851	CLK	1662	NWE	1555	HSY
1235	HSY	924	DON	690	CLK	854	BFD	1663	NWE	1556	COP
1236	DON	925	HSY	691	LIN	913	BFD	1664	NWE	1557	HSY

The GNR 2-4-0 which had carried no.1000 from new in June 1895, was altered on 16th February 1920 by the addition of the letter A, to clear 1000 for the first of Gresley's large boilered 2-6-0 type which became class K3.

On the Great Central, B was the letter added to show inclusion in Duplicate Stock, no.31 getting it in July 1922, which cleared 31 for a new 4-6-0 engine.

Having been superseded from working London suburban passenger trains, no.1511 had moved to Colwick, where it is being coaled. Note the blanking-off of the condensing apparatus it had needed for work in London district, but it still has destination board brackets.

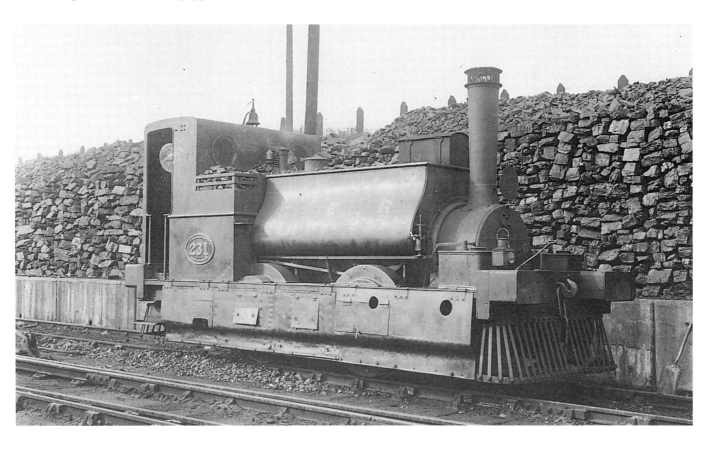

Colchester's 0-4-0 tank no.231 worked the Hythe quayside line from that shed, whose distinctive coal stack provided ready indication of the location.

1558	HSY
1559	HSY
1560	BFD
1561	HSY
1562	HSY
1563	KX
1564	BFD
1565	HSY
1566	COP
1567	KX
1568	BFD
1569	BFD
1570	KX
1571	HSY
1572	BFD
1573	HSY
1574	BFD
1575	HSY
1576	HSY
1577	HSY
1578	HSY
1579	KX
1580	HSY
1581	KX
1582	KX
1583	KX
1584	HSY
1585	HSY
1586	HSY
1588	HSY
1589	KX
1591	HSY
1592	COP
1593	BFD
1594	BFD
1595	BFD
1596	KX
1597	KX
1598	HSY
1599	KX
1600	KX
1601	KX
1602	KX
1603	KX
1604	KX
1605	KX

N2 (60)

1606	KX
1607	KX
1608	KX
1609	KX
1610	KX
1611	KX
1612	KX
1613	KX
1614	KX
1615	KX
1721	KX
1722	KX
1723	KX
1724	KX
1725	KX

1726	KX
1727	KX
1728	KX
1729	KX
1730	KX
1731	KX
1732	KX
1733	KX
1734	KX
1735	KX
1736	KX
1737	KX
1738	KX
1739	KX
1740	KX
1741	KX
1742	KX
1743	KX
1744	KX
1745	KX
1746	KX
1747	KX
1748	KX
1749	KX
1750	KX
1751	HSY
1752	HSY
1753	HSY
1754	HSY
1755	HSY
1756	KX
1757	KX
1758	KX
1759	HAT
1760	HAT
1761	HAT
1762	HAT
1763	HAT
1764	HIT
1765	KX
1766	KX
1767	KX
1768	HSY
1769	KX
1770	KX

O1 (20)

456	NWE
457	NWE
458	NWE
459	NWE
460	NWE
462	NWE
463	NWE
464	CLK
465	NWE
466	NWE
467	NWE
468	NWE
469	CLK
470	CLK
471	CLK
472	NWE

473	NWE
474	NWE
475	NWE
476	NWE

O2 (11)

461	NWE
477	NWE
478	NWE
479	NWE
480	NWE
481	NWE
482	NWE
483	NWE
484	NWE
485	NWE
486	NWE

Q1 (40)

401	CLK
403	DON
404	NWE
408	CLK
409	CLK
411	CLK
412	CLK
413	ARD
414	CLK
415	CLK
418	CLK
419	ARD
422	NWE
423	NWE
424	NWE
425	CLK
426	CLK
427	CLK
428	ARD
429	NWE
430	NWE
431	NWE
432	NWE
433	NWE
434	NWE
435	NWE
436	CLK
437	CLK
438	DON
439	CLK
440	NWE
441	NWE
442	NWE
443	CLK
444	ARD
445	ARD
446	NWE
447	NWE
448	CLK
449	CLK

Q2 (14)

402	CLK
405	ARD
406	ARD
407	ARD
410	CLK
416	CLK
417	CLK
421	CLK
450	CLK
451	CLK
452	NWE
453	DON
454	NWE
455	DON

Q3 (1)

420	NWE

R1 (41)

116	CLK
117	KX
118	CLK
119	CLK
120	CLK
121	CLK
122	CLK
123	CLK
124	CLK
125	KX
126	CLK
127	CLK
128	CLK
129	CLK
130	CLK
131	CLK
132	CLK
133	CLK
134	CLK
135	CLK
136	CLK
137	KX
138	CLK
139	CLK
140	CLK
141	CLK
142	CLK
143	CLK
144	CLK
145	CLK
146	CLK
147	CLK
148	CLK
149	CLK
150	CLK
151	KX
152	CLK
153	CLK
154	KX
155	CLK
156	KX

Unclassified (2)

533A 0-4-4CT
at DON Works
470A 0-6-0ST
at Hall Hills SD

_GN of SR_ 122

D38 (3)

75	KIT
76	KIT
77	KIT

D39 (3)

1	KIT
2	KEI
3	ELG

D40 (21)

25	KIT
26	KEI
27	KEI
28	KIT
29	KEI
31	KIT
33	KIT
34	KIT
35	KIT
36	KIT
45	KIT
46	KIT
47	KIT
48	KIT
49	KIT
50	KIT
52	KIT
54	ELG
113	KEI
114	KIT
115	KIT

D41 (32)

19	KIT
20	KIT
21	KIT
22	KEI
23	KEI
24	KIT
78	KEI
79	KIT
80	KEI
81	KIT
82	KIT
83	KIT
93	KIT
94	KEI
95	ELG
96	KIT
97	KIT
98	KIT
99	KEI
100	KIT
101	ELG
102	KIT
103	KIT
104	KIT

105	KEI
106	KIT
107	KIT
108	KIT
109	ELG
110	KIT
111	KIT
112	ELG

D42 (9)

4	ELG
7	KIT
9	KEI
10	KIT
17	ELG
18	KIT
72	KIT
73	KIT
74	KIT

D43 (3)

12	KIT
13	KIT
14	KIT

D44 (6)

63	ELG
64	KIT
65	ELG
66	KIT
67	KIT
68	KIT

D45 (9)

40	KIT
51	ELG
53	ELG
57	KIT
58	ELG
59	KIT
60	KIT
61	KIT
62	ELG

D46 (2)

5	KIT
6	KIT

D47 (9)

44A	KIT
45A	KIT
48A	KIT
49A	KIT
50A	KIT
52A	KIT
54A	KIT
55	KIT
56	KIT

D48 (3)

69	KIT
70	KIT
71	KEI

G10 (9)

84	KIT
85	KIT
86	KIT
87	KIT
88	KIT
89	KIT
90	KIT
91	KIT
92	KIT

J90 (6)

8	KIT
11	KIT
15	KIT
16	KIT
39	KIT
42	KIT

J91 (3)

37	KIT
38	KIT
41	KIT

Z4 (2)

43	KIT
44	KIT

Z5 (2)

30	KIT
32	KIT

***NBR* 1074**

C10 (6)

901	STM
902	DEE
903	STM
904	STM
905	CAR
906	CAR

C11 (16)

509	DEE
510	STM
868	DEE
869	DEE
870	ABD
871	ABD
872	ABD
873	HAY
874	HAY
875	HAY
876	HAY
877	HAY
878	CAR
879	CAR
880	CAR
881	CAR

C15 (30)

1	HAY
2	PKD
3	PKD
4	KPS
5	PKD
6	EFD
12	STM
15	DFU
16	PKD
25	HAY
26	DFU
39	THJ
41	STM
43	STM
48	STM
51	PKD
53	STM
64	PKD
102	PKD
122	EFD
131	EFD
133	STM
134	STM
135	STM
141	HAY
155	EFD
164	PKD
265	EFD
267	KPS
309	KPS

C16 (21)

438	KPS
439	EFD
440	PKD
441	EFD
442	EFD
443	PKD
444	PKD
445	PKD
446	KPS
447	KPS
448	STM
449	STM
450	STM
451	STM
452	STM
511	STM
512	KPS
513	EFD
514	EFD
515	EFD
516	EFD

D25 (12)

592	STG
593	DFU
594	EFD
595	HAY
596	HAY
597	HAY
598	DEE
599	HAW
600	EFD
601	STG
602	EFD
603	EFD

D26 (9)

317	STM
318	STM
320	STM
322	DEE
323	STM
324	STM
325	STM
326	STM
327	DEE

D27 (3)

1321	EFD
1323	HAY
1324	HAY

D28 (4)

1322	EFD
1361	HAY
1387	HAY
1388	EFD

D29 (16)

243	PTH
244	PTH
245	DEE
338	HAY
339	HAY
340	ABD
359	DEE
360	CAR
361	HAY
362	DEE
895	STM
896	DEE
897	STM
898	HAW
899	STM
900	STM

D30 (27)

363	STM
400	STM
409	PTH
410	EFD
411	EFD
412	CAR
413	HAY
414	HAY
415	HAY
416	HAY
417	STM
418	PTH
419	DEE
420	DEE
421	DEE
422	DEE
423	STM
424	HAY
425	DEE
426	STM
427	CAR
428	HAY
497	EFD
498	EFD
499	EFD
500	EFD
501	EFD

D31 (48)

36	CAR
37	STG
211	HAY
212	HAY
213	STM
214	PTH
215	PKD
216	CAR
217	EFD
218	CAR
262	DFU
293	EFD
312	BLA (NE)

404	HAW
574	PTH
575	BGT
576	HAW
577	STM
578	BGT
579	HAY
633	HAW
634	PTH
635	THJ
636	THJ
637	PTH
638	EFD
639	BGT
640	DFU
641	DFU
642	HAY
729	HAY
730	HAY
731	PTH
732	STM
733	HAY
734	HAY
735	HAY
736	HAY
737	STM
738	PTH
739	ABD
740	STM
765	DEE
766	STM
767	THJ
768	EFD
769	STG
770	THJ

D32 (12)

882	STM
883	STM
884	STM
885	DEE
886	DEE
887	BWK
888	BWK
889	STM
890	STM
891	STM
892	BWK
893	THJ

D33 (12)

331	STM
332	EFD
333	THJ
382	DEE
383	THJ
384	THJ
385	THJ
864	THJ
865	BWK
866	DEE
867	THJ

D33 cont.

894	STM

D34 (32)

34	THJ
35	THJ
100	EFD
149	THJ
153	EFD
221	EFD
241	EFD
242	EFD
256	EFD
258	EFD
266	STM
270	PTH
278	STM
281	EFD
287	STM
291	HAY
298	EFD
307	EFD
405	EFD
406	EFD
407	EFD
408	EFD
490	EFD
492	STM
493	EFD
494	EFD
495	EFD
496	EFD
502	STM
503	STM
504	STM
505	DEE

D35 (7)

1434	DFU
1439	HAY
1442	EFD
1448	EFD
1449	EFD
1452	BGT
1453	EFD

D36 (1)

695	PKD

D50 (3)

1390	EFD
1391	DEE
1392	BGT

D51 (30)

1401	Roth
1402	RDS
1404	STG
1405	BGT

1406	DEE
1411	STM
1424	STM
1425	STM
1426	STG
1427	POL
1428	STM
1429	EFD
1454	EFD
1455	STG
1456	STM
1457	BGT
1458	DFU
1459	POL
1460	POL
1461	KPS
1462	HAW
1463	PTH
1464	KPS
1465	DEE
1466	STM
1467	STM
1468	STM
1469	STM
1470	STM
1471	BTD

E7 (6)

1239	DFU
1245	BWK
1246	BWK
1247	DFU
1249	BTD
1256	BWK

G7 (12)

90	HAW
91	STM
92	DFU
93	CAR
94	DFU
95	PKD
586	KPS
587	POL
588	PKD
589	PTH
590	EFD
591	STG

G8 (6)

1320	DEE
1325	DEE
1326	STG
1327	STM
1334	DEE
1338	DEE

G9 (12)

239	KPS
334	STM

349	DEE
350	DEE
351	DEE
352	DEE
353	STM
354	STM
355	DEE
356	PKD
474	STG
475	KPS

J31 (37)

1070	HAY
1082	STM
1114	THJ
1122	BTD
1132	CAR
1133	HAW
1134	BWK
1137	HAW
1138	BGT
1140	EFD
1141	STG
1142	STG
1143	STM
1144	STG
1146	STM
1147	HAW
1148	HAW
1149	HAW
1162	DFU
1164	KPS
1166	DFU
1178	STM
1180	HAW
1183	PKD
1188	BTD
1189	DFU
1190	POL
1195	BWK
1200	STM
1206	STG
1208	KPS
1214	PKD
1221	CAR
1223	DFU
1224	CAR
1227	STM
1296	THJ

J32 (19)

1297	POL
1298	KPS
1300	HAW
1304	PKD
1305	POL
1310	THJ
1311	CAR
1312	KPS
1314	HAY
1315	HAY
1319	STM

1329	PKD
1337	KPS
1339	KPS
1341	STM
1343	HAY
1344	EFD
1345	EFD
1346	EFD

J33 (36)

21	BTD
24	RDS
80	KPS
81	STM
82	STM
83	PKD
85	STM
112	DFU
137	BGT
140	BGT
148	BTD
150	KPS
156	PKD
159	DFU
160	THJ
168	POL
169	POL
170	EFD
178	BTD
249	STM
269	STM
484	PKD
566	HAW
567	STM
568	STM
569	HAW
570	CAR
571	PKD
572	STM
573	CAR
580	POL
581	POL
582	KPS
583	KPS
584	KPS
585	KPS

J34 (93)

18	PKD
27	BGT
28	BGT
30	BTD
125	BGT
138	BGT
163	BTD
184	PKD
286	STM
311	POL
481	THJ
482	PKD
527	STM
529	BTD

530	BGT
531	EFD
532	KPS
533	BTD
534	BGT
535	EFD
536	KPS
537	POL
538	BGT
539	EFD
540	DFU
541	BTD
542	PKD
543	DEE
544	HAW
545	POL
548	KPS
549	PKD
550	POL
551	BTD
552	PKD
553	DEE
554	ABD
555	POL
556	HAW
557	KPS
558	DFU
559	DFU
560	DFU
561	BTD
562	KPS
563	EFD
564	BGT
565	HAY
1364	EFD
1365	THJ
1366	EFD
1367	DFU
1368	KPS
1369	THJ
1370	THJ
1377	EFD
1380	BGT
1381	BGT
1383	EFD
1386	EFD
1393	DFU
1394	PKD
1395	STG
1396	POL
1397	DFU
1400	STG
1407	KPS
1409	BGT
1410	THJ
1412	KPS
1413	ABD
1414	EFD
1415	THJ
1416	THJ
1417	PKD
1418	BGT
1419	BGT
1420	BTD

1421	PTH
1422	STM
1423	STM
1430	CAR
1431	BGT
1432	DFU
1472	BGT
1473	THJ
1474	BTD
1475	KPS
1476	THJ
1477	BGT
1478	DFU
1479	BGT
1481	POL

J35 (76)

38	THJ
56	PTH
57	EFD
58	DEE
59	STM
86	POL
115	KPS
120	DFU
124	STM
126	STM
127	EFD
129	STM
185	EFD
186	CAR
187	STM
188	STM
189	CAR
190	STM
191	BWK
192	STM
193	DFU
194	DEE
195	DEE
196	DFU
197	DEE
198	DEE
199	STM
200	PTH
201	BGT
202	EFD
203	POL
204	BGT
205	STM
206	BWK
207	DEE
208	DEE
220	CAR
226	CAR
228	DEE
253	BGT
254	DEE
329	EFD
330	EFD
335	DEE
336	THJ
337	DEE

347	STM	618	DEE	692	STM	786	STM	306	EFD	1328	PKD
348	STG	619	STM	705	THJ	787	EFD	313	BWK	1330	PTH
364	DEE	620	THJ	706	EFD	788	STM	314	BWK	1331	EFD
365	STM	621	KPS	707	ABD	789	STM	315	DEE	1332	THJ
366	THJ	622	KPS	708	POL	790	STM	401	EFD	1333	BWK
367	CAR	623	PKD	709	BGT	791	Roth	402	DFU	1335	DFU
368	THJ	624	RDS	710	BGT	792	STG	403	EFD	1336	HAY
369	STM	625	CAR	711	STM	793	THJ	429	STM	1348	CAR
370	DEE	626	BGT	712	PKD	794	BTD	430	DEE	1349	CAR
371	PKD	627	STM	713	STM			431	DEE	1350	STM
372	EFD	628	DFU	714	KPS	**J37** (104)		432	EFD	1351	BWK
373	HAY	629	STM	715	STM			433	POL	1352	EFD
374	BGT	630	BGT	716	BGT	8	EFD	434	EFD	1353	PTH
375	THJ	631	EFD	717	STM	13	ABD	435	BWK	1354	EFD
376	DEE	632	THJ	718	KPS	33	EFD	436	CAR	1355	THJ
377	KPS	643	BTD	719	THJ	44	EFD	437	EFD	1356	PTH
378	BGT	644	POL	720	THJ	46	BWK	454	CAR	1357	STM
379	STM	645	EFD	721	EFD	62	EFD	455	CAR	1358	STM
380	PKD	646	POL	722	STM	72	STM	456	EFD	1359	THJ
381	BGT	647	KPS	723	BGT	73	STM	457	PKD		
848	HAY	648	STM	724	HEX (NE)	84	STM	458	CAR	**J83** (40)	
849	EFD	649	DEE	725	THJ	88	STM	459	CAR		
850	STM	650	THJ	726	PTH	89	STM	460	ABD	795	KPS
851	STM	651	EFD	727	PKD	98	EFD	461	ABD	796	KPS
852	THJ	652	EFD	728	PKD	101	CAR	462	BWK	797	KPS
853	STM	653	BGT	741	STG	103	EFD	463	EFD	798	KPS
854	STM	654	BGT	742	HAW	104	STM	464	PKD	799	PKD
855	DFU	655	EFD	743	EFD	105	STM	465	EFD	800	EFD
856	EFD	656	STM	744	EFD	109	STM	466	BWK	801	STM
857	EFD	657	POL	745	STG	110	DEE	467	THJ	802	CAR
		658	STM	746	HAW	111	DEE	468	KPS	803	STM
J36 (168)		659	THJ	747	POL	113	EFD	469	THJ	804	THJ
		660	STM	748	STM	123	BWK	470	STM	805	DEE
45	POL	661	DFU	749	EFD	128	STM	471	STM	806	THJ
68	KPS	662	DFU	750	EFD	136	ABD	472	STM	807	STM
145	DFU	663	EFD	751	DEE	139	STM	473	STM	808	DEE
172	PKD	664	THJ	752	EFD	143	STM	476	ABD	809	THJ
173	THJ	665	EFD	753	STM	151	STM	477	DEE	810	CAR
176	DFU	666	BGT	754	RDS	157	STM	478	PTH	811	THJ
177	PKD	667	THJ	755	KPS	158	STM	479	DEE	812	DFU
179	DEE	668	PTH	756	STM	161	BLA (NE)	480	BWK	813	HAY
180	KPS	669	POL	757	STM	162	DFU	485	ABD	814	PKD
181	BGT	670	STG	758	STM	167	DFU	486	ABD	815	DEE
182	BGT	671	BGT	759	STM	171	EFD	487	KPS	816	STM
183	DFU	672	STM	760	KPS	175	EFD	488	THJ	817	STM
247	EFD	673	PKD	761	EFD	222	CAR	489	DEE	818	EFD
248	DFU	674	PKD	762	BTD	255	STM	491	BWK	819	DEE
250	BGT	675	DEE	763	KPS	260	EFD	506	EFD	820	THJ
280	EFD	676	STM	764	STG	261	POL	507	EFD	821	EFD
357	THJ	677	BTD	771	DFU	263	EFD	508	EFD	822	PTH
358	STM	678	STM	772	PKD	272	EFD	517	DEE	823	EFD
604	EFD	679	STM	773	KPS	273	EFD	518	EFD	824	POL
605	HAW	680	STM	774	DEE	274	BWK			825	STM
606	POL	681	DFU	775	STM	292	ABD	**J81** (1)		826	HAY
607	CAR	682	BTD	776	DEE	295	ABD			827	STM
608	STM	683	BGT	777	POL	296	DEE	1216	PKD	828	HAY
609	DEE	684	STM	778	DEE	297	EFD			829	EFD
611	POL	685	KPS	779	RDS	299	EFD	**J82** (24)		830	STM
612	THJ	686	POL	780	THJ	300	EFD			831	DFU
613	STG	687	STM	781	STM	301	BWK	1289	POL	832	EFD
614	STM	688	STM	782	STM	302	BWK	1291	STM	833	EFD
615	BGT	689	KPS	783	EFD	303	EFD	1294	POL	834	EFD
616	BTD	690	BGT	784	EFD	304	POL	1299	STG		
617	DEE	691	CAR	785	THJ	305	BWK	1306	EFD		

J84 (3)

1257	KPS
1259	PKD
1270	STM

J85 (1)

1168	EFD

J86 (1)

1173	POL

J88 (35)

66	STM
87	DEE
114	STM
116	STM
117	BTD
118	THJ
119	BTD
121	KPS
130	EFD
132	KPS
152	EFD
233	THJ
234	EFD
235	STM
236	THJ
237	EFD
238	THJ
271	STG
277	HAY
279	STM
288	STM
289	PKD
290	EFD
836	BTD
837	BTD
838	THJ
839	BTD
840	POL
841	STM
842	PKD
843	PTH
844	HAY
845	KPS
846	STM
847	THJ

N14 (6)

858	EFD
859	EFD
860	EFD
861	EFD
862	EFD
863	STM

N15 (69)

7	STM
20	STM
22	STM
29	BGT
47	STM
49	ABD
54	STM
61	BTD
65	BTD
69	EFD
70	ABD
96	THJ
97	BGT
106	THJ
107	BGT
108	PKD
142	EFD
154	EFD
165	EFD
166	EFD
209	THJ
210	THJ
219	THJ
223	EFD
224	EFD
229	EFD
230	STM
240	PKD
246	STM
251	EFD
252	STM
257	KPS
259	EFD
264	KPS
276	EFD
282	EFD
386	BGT
387	HAY
388	STM
389	DFU
390	DFU
391	POL
392	EFD
393	PKD
396	KPS
397	KPS
398	BGT
399	BGT
453	EFD
907	STM
908	STM
909	STM
910	STM
911	BWK
912	STM
913	THJ
914	BTD
915	THJ
916	THJ
917	DFU
918	DFU
919	KPS
920	EFD
921	BGT
922	BGT
923	BGT
924	BGT
925	POL
926	EFD

Y9 (35)

9	POL
10	STM
11	KPS
14	KPS
17	POL
32	POL
40	DFU
42	STM
50	EFD
63	KPS
144	EFD
146	STM
308	EFD
310	EFD
546	STM
547	EFD
610	EFD
1083	STM
1084	DEE
1087	EFD
1088	KPS
1089	STM
1090	STM
1091	KPS
1092	DEE
1093	KPS
1094	KPS
1095	STM
1096	EFD
1097	STM
1098	DEE
1100	STM
1101	STM
1102	STM
1103	POL

Y10 (1)

1011	KPS

NER 2143

A2 (2)

2400	GHD
2401	GHD

A6 (10)

686	NEV
687	SALT
688	WBY
689	WBY
690	SALT
691	WBY
692	WBY
693	SCA
694	SCA
695	MAL

A7 (20)

1113	YK
1114	THK
1126	HLD
1129	SDN
1136	SEL
1170	SBK
1174	SDN
1175	HLD
1176	THK
1179	SKN
1180	SDN
1181	WHL
1182	SBK
1183	SDN
1185	SBK
1190	SKN
1191	WHL
1192	YK
1193	SBK
1195	SDN

B13 (40)

726	HLD
738	TWD
739	TWD
740	HLD
741	TWD
743	NEV
744	HLD
745	TWD
746	HLD
747	TWD
748	HLD
749	HLD
750	NEV
751	HLD
752	HTN
753	NEV
754	TWD
755	HLD
756	BLA
757	HTN
758	HLD
759	HTN
760	HLD
761	HTN
762	NEV
763	HLD
766	BLA
768	HLD
775	BLA
1077	HTN
2001	TWD
2002	HTN
2003	HTN
2004	HLD
2005	HTN
2006	NEV
2007	TWD
2008	NEV
2009	HLD
2010	HLD

B14 (5)

2111	GHD
2112	GHD
2113	GHD
2114	GHD
2115	GHD

B15 (20)

782	HTN
786	HLD
787	HTN
788	HTN
791	HTN
795	HTN
796	HTN
797	HTN
798	HTN
799	YK
813	SCA
815	DON (GN)
817	YK
819	NEV
820	YK
821	YK
822	YK
823	YK
824	DAR
825	HTN

B16 (38)

840	HTN
841	HTN
842	HTN
843	HTN
844	YK
845	YK
846	HTN
847	YK
848	YK
849	YK
906	HTN
908	YK
909	TWD
911	YK
914	HTN
915	YK
920	GHD
921	YK
922	HTN
923	YK
924	TWD
925	YK
926	TWD
927	YK
928	TWD
929	NEV
930	HTN
931	NEV
932	HTN
933	YK
934	HTN
936	YK
937	HTN
942	YK
943	HTN
2363	GHD
2364	YK
2365	GHD

C6 (20)

295	GHD
532	HTN
649	HTN
696	GHD
697	TWD
698	YK
699	YK
700	TWD
701	GHD
702	YK
703	TWD
704	GHD
705	GHD
742	HTN
784	HTN
1680	HTN
1753	GHD
1776	HTN
1792	YK
1794	GHD

C7 (50)

706	GHD
709	GHD
710	HTN
714	HAY (NE)
716	GHD
717	GHD
718	GHD
719	GHD
720	GHD

721 GHD	1631 GHD	1026 YK	**D22** (37)	**D24** (5)	128 SUN
722 GHD	1632 TWD	1042 DAR			155 SUN
727 GHD	1633 HLB	1051 GHD	18 ALN	3033 HLS	169 SBH
728 GHD	1634 TWD	1078 HTN	42 HLB	3035 HLS	172 TDK
729 GHD	1635 HLB	1147 GHD	85 HLB	3038 HLS	187 HLB
732 GHD	1636 GHD	1184 GHD	96 HLB	3041 HLS	201 MAL
733 GHD	1637 ALN	1206 GHD	115 BRI	3042 HLS	205 SKN
734 GHD	1638 GHD	1207 HTN	117 BRI		262 HLS
735 GHD	1639 HLB	1209 GHD	154 CAR	**E5** (20)	279 NLT
736 GHD		1210 TWD	194 HLB		404 TDK
737 GHD	**D17/2** (30)	1217 DAR	230 BRI	1463 DAR	414 SBH
2163 YK		1223 GHD	340 HLB	1464 KBS	415 SKN
2164 YK	1871 WHL	1232 HTN	355 CAR	1465 KBS	418 NLT
2165 YK	1872 WHL	1234 HLB	356 SCA	1466 SCA	419 MAL
2166 YK	1873 WHL	1235 GHD	514 BRI	1467 DAR	420 MID
2167 YK	1874 SCA	1236 GHD	663 WAS	1468 HLD	423 GHD
2168 YK	1875 NEV	1258 GHD	673 SEL	1469 BCas	425 TWD
2169 YK	1876 CAR	1260 YK	684 BRI	1470 DAR	454 NBH
2170 GHD	1877 NEV	1665 GHD	777 HLB	1471 SCA	469 NLT
2171 YK	1878 SCA	1672 YK	779 SCA	1472 SEL	483 TWD
2172 YK	1879 WHL	2011 NEV	803 HLB	1473 KBS	485 ALN
2193 HAY (NE)	1880 GHD	2012 BLA	808 HLS	1474 DAR	490 WBY
2194 HAY (NE)	1901 CAR	2013 NEV	1137 HLB	1475 DAR	507 SBH
2195 HTN	1902 SCA	2014 HLB	1324 CAR	1476 MID	537 WBY
2196 HTN	1903 SCA	2015 TWD	1532 SEL	1477 SALT	575 NBH
2197 HTN	1904 WHL	2016 GHD	1533 SBK	1478 ALN	671 TDK
2198 YK	1905 NEV	2017 TWD	1534 HLB	1479 YK	674 NEV
2199 YK	1906 SCA	2018 YK	1535 SEL	1504 ALN	685 MID
2200 HTN	1907 SCA	2019 DAR	1536 BRI	1505 WHL	801 NEV
2201 NEV	1908 WHL	2020 NEV	1537 SEL	1506 MID	804 GHD
2202 YK	1909 GHD	2021 YK	1538 HLS		854 MID
2203 HTN	1910 CAR	2022 YK	1539 BRI	**'901'** (10)	1160 ALN
2204 HAY (NE)	1921 CAR	2023 DAR	1540 HLB		1171 TDK
2205 GHD	1922 SBK	2024 TWD	1541 SCA	19 PEN	1322 HLB
2206 HTN	1923 NEV	2025 TWD	1542 SCA	53 DAR	1577 WBY
2207 NEV	1924 CAR	2026 NEV	1543 HLB	269 BCas	1578 SUN
2208 YK	1925 CAR	2027 YK	1544 SEL	363 BCas	1579 WBY
2209 GHD	1926 CAR	2028 YK	1545 SBK	366 BCas	1580 MAL
2210 NEV	1927 GHD	2029 TWD	1546 GHD	367 BCas	1581 MAL
2211 HTN	1928 CAR	2030 GHD		370 MinT	1582 HLB
2212 GHD	1929 CAR	2101 YK	**D23** (20)	464 BCas	1583 WBY
	1930 WHL	2102 HLB		910 YK	1584 NEV
C8 (2)		2103 HLB	23 HLB	1325 KBS	1585 TDK
	D18 (2)	2104 YK	214 MAL		1586 HEX
730 GHD		2105 GHD	217 SCA	**'1440'** (9)	1597 MID
731 GHD	1869 NEV	2106 DAR	222 HLB		1598 HAV
	1870 NEV	2107 GHD	223 HLB	150 TWD	1599 MAS
'38' (1)		2108 NEV	258 HLB	220 ALN	1600 TDK
	D19 (1)	2109 NEV	274 SBK	486 YK	1601 MID
281 YK		2110 DAR	328 BFD	1441 DUR	1602 NEV
	1619 HLB		337 HLB	1442 DUR	1603 NLT
D17/1 (20)		**D21** (10)	372 DAR	1443 DUR	1604 TWD
	D20 (60)		472 SCA	1446 DUR	1605 TDK
1620 DON (GN)		1237 YK	521 HLB	1448 DUR	1606 HAV
1621 GHD	476 DAR	1238 YK	557 HLB	1449 KBS	
1622 HLB	592 TWD	1239 YK	675 HLB		**G5** (110)
1623 HLB	707 YK	1240 YK	676 HLB	**F8** (60)	
1624 TWD	708 YK	1241 YK	677 HLB		149 SBK
1625 GHD	711 YK	1242 SBK	678 SBK	21 TWD	380 WHL
1626 HLB	712 HLB	1243 NEV	679 HLB	35 ALS	381 SCA
1627 TWD	713 YK	1244 NEV	1107 SCA	40 NLT	384 HTN
1628 HLB	723 TWD	1245 YK	1120 SBK	41 WAUK	387 SUN
1629 HLB	724 YK	1246 YK		55 TWD	394 MAL
1630 HLB	725 NEV			72 NEV	405 HEX

Here is evidence that the North Eastern did have a steam engine with no.1, carried also on a brass plate, but of much more impressive size. In January 1914, that number was changed to 356.

0-6-0 tank 1155 not only had a B cast on its number plate but, for good measure, also carried it more prominently by a shaded transfer.

Cast plates showing Duplicate List numbering could also be seen on the Great Eastern, this 0-4-0 tram engine having the cypher from March 1921 when 129 was taken by a new 0-6-0 tram engine.

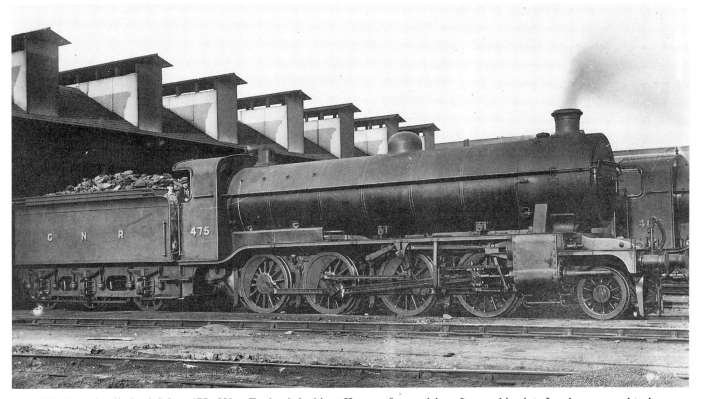

Great Northern 2-cylinder 2-8-0 no.475 of New England shed is at Hornsey for servicing after working into London on a coal train.

No.	Shed	No.	Shed	No.	Shed	No.	Shed	No.	Shed	No.	Shed
408	STH	1882	FYL	353	NBH	2155	GHD	530	SUN	1336	HTN
413	WHL	1883	SBH	358	SBK	2156	GHD	534	YK	1337	BLA
427	FYL	1884	NEV	416	HTN	2157	HTN	538	HTN	1338	BLA
433	WHL	1885	SUN	465	SUN	2158	HTN	539	HTN	1339	TWD
435	HLB	1886	HTN	466	YK	2159	HTN	556	SBK	1507	SDN
436	HLB	1887	SKN	585	SBH	2160	HTN	558	HTN	1508	HTN
437	SUN	1888	PKG	588	HAWJ	2161	SBK	564	WHL	1509	DAR
439	SBK	1889	MID	595	SBH	2162	SALT	568	CAR	1510	HTN
441	SUN	1890	SKN	605	CAR			569	HTN	1511	SKN
468	DAR	1911	THK	615	SBK	**J21** (201)		570	CAR	1512	DAR
505	MAL	1912	SBK	624	CAR			579	SBK	1513	HLD
526	MID	1913	WHL	638	WHL	16	WAUK	582	DAR	1514	SUN
529	SBK	1914	WBY	672	SEL	22	SBK	611	DAR	1515	THK
540	WHL	1915	SBK	947	SBH	26	MID	613	WHL	1516	YK
580	NEV	1916	GHD	949	WAUK	30	SKN	619	NEV	1547	SKN
1096	NEV	1917	SUN	950	SBH	31	HTN	665	HLD	1548	HLD
1169	BLA	1918	HTN	951	YK	34	YK	666	CAR	1549	SBK
1316	HTN	1919	SUN	952	NBH	48	WHL	667	HTN	1550	SDN
1319	WBY	1920	GHD	955	GHD	51	GHD	668	KBS	1551	SUN
1334	HLB	2081	SUN	1019	WHL	56	SUN	680	HLD	1552	MID
1687	HTN	2082	WHL	1020	GSB	68	MID	776	SUN	1553	WVJ
1691	BLA	2083	SUN	1055	SALT	86	HLD	778	HLD	1554	SEL
1692	SUN	2084	CAR	1312	YK	93	SDN	800	KBS	1555	WHL
1693	SUN	2085	WHL	1436	SBH	95	NBH	806	NEV	1556	DAR
1695	WHL	2086	HTN			97	HLD	807	YK	1557	BLA
1701	SCA	2087	SKN	**H1** (45)		99	SDN	810	HLD	1558	WHL
1702	BLA	2088	PKG			101	SUN	869	SUN	1559	TDK
1703	HLB	2089	Rich	1326	NEV	102	HLD	871	HTN	1560	WHL
1713	WHL	2090	SBK	1327	DAR	104	CAR	872	CAR	1561	MID
1730	SUN	2091	SBK	1328	BLA	107	GHD	874	HLD	1562	CAR
1737	SDN	2092	SBK	1329	BLA	110	SDN	875	WHL	1563	ALN
1739	WBY	2093	GHD	1330	BLA	122	NBH	876	WHL	1564	BLA
1740	SKN	2094	HEX	1499	HTN	123	TDK	877	HTN	1565	HTN
1745	HTN	2095	GHD	1500	SBK	133	NBH	878	SUN	1566	DAR
1748	HTN	2096	HTN	1501	HTN	139	MID	899	WHL	1567	NEV
1751	BLA	2097	CAR	1502	DAR	147	SKN	944	SDN	1568	HLD
1752	SUN	2098	SUN	1503	DAR	148	SKN	960	HTN	1569	NEV
1754	HTN	2099	SUN	1517	GHD	152	TWD	962	HTN	1570	MID
1755	HTN	2100	GHD	1518	NEV	157	MID	963	HLD	1571	HLD
1759	SUN			1519	HTN	160	SUN	965	BLA	1572	HLD
1762	HTN	**G6** (46)		1520	SBK	182	HTN	973	SEL	1573	SKN
1764	SKN			1521	BLA	209	SKN	974	HTN	1574	SKN
1765	HEX	60	CAR	1522	BLA	259	GHD	975	WHL	1575	DAR
1769	SUN	62	HTN	1523	HTN	289	MID	976	HLD	1576	HTN
1772	SUN	63	SALT	1524	DAR	291	HLD	979	SKN	1587	WHL
1775	SBK	65	MID	1525	DAR	294	HLD	981	HLD	1588	BLA
1778	SUN	87	SCA	1526	DAR	300	NEV	992	HTN	1589	SKN
1779	MID	91	SALT	1527	DAR	312	SKN	993	HLD	1590	HLD
1780	WHL	92	WHL	1528	SBK	313	GHD	994	HTN	1591	WHL
1783	BLA	108	NEV	1529	HTN	314	WHL	996	SDN	1592	MID
1786	MID	189	SEL	1530	SBK	315	BLA	997	DAR	1593	MID
1788	GHD	226	MID	1531	NEV	316	HLD	1071	HTN	1594	MID
1791	HTN	247	HLB	2143	NEV	331	HLD	1073	SKN	1595	DAR
1793	HTN	255	YK	2144	SALT	360	HTN	1075	DAR	1596	NEV
1795	MID	256	HTN	2145	SALT	424	HTN	1122	BLA	1607	BLA
1837	SUN	273	CAR	2146	SALT	431	HLD	1161	SBH	1608	HTN
1838	TWD	288	YK	2147	NEV	432	MID	1187	HTN	1609	BLA
1839	PatB	297	PKG	2148	SALT	458	BLA	1188	BLA	1610	BLA
1840	BLA	321	SUN	2149	SALT	470	SBK	1301	BLA	1611	BLA
1865	HTN	322	CAR	2150	SALT	480	HTN	1305	WHL	1612	HLD
1866	TWD	323	HTN	2151	SALT	510	SBK	1309	HTN	1613	BLA
1867	HEX	334	SBK	2152	SALT	511	CAR	1315	DAR	1614	GHD
1868	BLA	341	HLB	2153	GHD	513	HTN	1323	SDN	1615	TWD
1881	WRH	343	MID	2154	GHD	520	SKN	1332	SUN	1616	NBH

1801 HTN	1489 DAR	**J24** (70)	1953 NPT	2031 SUN	2140 CAR
1802 CAR	1490 FYL		1954 MID	2032 NLT	2141 BOR
1803 YK	1491 NPT	1821 DAR	1955 BLA	2033 SUN	2142 THK
1804 YK		1822 NPT	1956 NPT	2034 NEV	
1805 NEV	**J23** (55)	1823 DAR	1957 NPT	2035 SEL	**J26** (50)
1806 NEV		1824 NLT	1958 MID	2036 SEL	
1807 YK	3049 CUD	1825 SKN	1959 SBH	2037 SEL	67 EHL
1808 SEL	3050 CUD	1826 PMN	1960 MID	2038 HLD	132 WHL
1809 YK	3051 CUD	1827 FYL		2039 SUN	233 WHL
1810 MID	3052 HLS	1828 BOR	**J25** (120)	2040 TDK	243 WHL
1811 GHD	3053 CUD	1829 SUN		2041 MID	342 HTN
1812 BLA	3054 HLS	1830 SBH	25 WVJ	2042 WAUK	379 PMN
1813 CAR	3055 BCJ	1841 BOR	29 SDN	2043 SDN	406 FYL
1814 NEV	3056 CUD	1842 SBH	257 CAR	2044 DAR	412 YK
1815 HLD	3057 CUD	1843 NBH	459 SKN	2045 WAUK	434 BLA
1816 HTN	3058 CUD	1844 YK	463 MID	2046 SDN	438 HAV
1817 GHD	3059 CUD	1845 NPT	536 ANP	2047 HLS	442 YK
1818 HTN	3060 HLS	1846 SUN	1714 GHD	2048 HLD	517 SBK
1819 GHD	3061 HLS	1847 PMN	1723 NEV	2049 SEL	525 YK
1820 ALN	3062 HLS	1848 TDK	1724 TDK	2050 SEL	543 NEV
	3063 HLS	1849 SALT	1725 TDK	2051 HLS	554 YK
J22 (44)	3064 HLS	1850 NLT	1726 DAR	2052 SEL	555 TDK
	3065 HLS	1851 NPT	1727 SUN	2053 SUN	765 MID
59 NPT	3066 HLS	1852 MID	1743 THK	2054 SDN	816 WHL
78 SBH	3070 CUD	1853 DAR	1961 NBH	2055 SEL	818 YK
131 NPT	3071 CUD	1854 BLA	1962 NBH	2056 NPT	831 YK
142 WBY	3072 HLS	1855 TDK	1963 NBH	2057 SEL	835 BOR
192 PKG	3073 HLS	1856 PMN	1964 NBH	2058 DAR	881 BOR
208 WBY	3074 HLS	1857 TDK	1965 SDN	2059 SDN	1043 WHL
232 FYL	3075 CUD	1858 TDK	1966 KBS	2060 WBY	1057 NPT
235 MAL	3076 HLS	1859 SUN	1967 WAUK	2061 WAUK	1098 YK
369 NPT	3077 HLS	1860 ROS	1968 NBH	2062 GHD	1130 YK
388 TDK	3078 HLS	1891 DAR	1969 SBH	2063 NBH	1131 NPT
422 HLD	3079 HLS	1892 SKN	1970 NEV	2064 SBH	1139 WHL
440 MAL	3080 DEN	1893 ROS	1971 SBH	2065 SUN	1146 HAV
446 WHL	3081 CUD	1894 SEL	1972 DAR	2066 NLT	1159 SEL
455 TWD	3082 CUD	1895 MID	1973 THK	2067 NEV	1172 NPT
491 SBK	3083 CUD	1896 SEL	1974 SEL	2068 THK	1194 HAV
497 SCA	3084 CUD	1897 MID	1975 DAR	2069 TDK	1200 YK
498 WAS	3085 CUD	1898 BOR	1976 SBH	2070 SEL	1202 HAV
502 DAR	3086 CUD	1899 NPT	1977 NEV	2071 PMN	1208 HAV
506 MAL	3087 CUD	1900 BOR	1978 WAUK	2072 WAUK	1360 WHL
508 MAL	3088 CUD	1931 DAR	1979 WAUK	2073 TDK	1366 YK
522 BOR	3089 HLS	1932 SBH	1980 WAUK	2074 WAUK	1369 BLA
565 ALN	3090 HLS	1933 NBH	1981 SUN	2075 CAR	1370 DAR
567 WAUK	3091 HLS	1934 BLA	1982 SUN	2076 TDK	1390 HAV
571 HLD	3092 HLS	1935 SBH	1983 TDK	2077 TDK	1670 WHL
606 DAR	3093 HLS	1936 DAR	1984 SUN	2078 WAUK	1671 NPT
620 FYL	3094 HLS	1937 BOR	1985 BLA	2079 WAUK	1673 WHL
681 SBH	3095 HLS	1938 BOR	1986 BOR	2080 MID	1674 YK
682 SCA	3096 HLS	1939 TDK	1987 NPT	2126 PMN	1676 TDK
812 MAL	3132 HLS	1940 NBH	1988 WAUK	2127 SUN	1678 NPT
1102 FYL	3133 HLS	1941 NPT	1989 THK	2128 SEL	1698 EHL
1106 MAL	3134 HLS	1942 NPT	1990 THK	2129 SCA	1773 SBK
1141 SCA	3135 HLS	1943 NPT	1991 THK	2130 MID	1777 NPT
1480 SKN	3136 HLS	1944 MID	1992 WAUK	2131 WAUK	1781 HAV
1481 BOR	3137 HLS	1945 MID	1993 ANP	2132 SDN	
1482 NBH	3138 HLS	1946 SUN	1994 KBS	2133 BOR	**J27** (105)
1483 DUR	3139 HLS	1947 MID	1995 WAUK	2134 SDN	
1484 DAR	3140 HLS	1948 SEL	1996 SUN	2135 NPT	790 CAR
1485 WBY	3141 HLS	1949 MID	1997 SUN	2136 SCA	814 NPT
1486 PMN		1950 ROS	1998 SBH	2137 BLA	836 SUN
1487 NBH		1951 DAR	1999 WAUK	2138 PMN	839 CAR
1488 SBH		1952 WBY	2000 BOR	2139 WAUK	880 PMN

No.	Depot	No.	Depot	No.	Depot	No.	Depot	No.	Depot	No.	Depot
883	SUN	1225	SDN	**'398'** (86)		1090	WVJ	286	HLA	1666	MID
888	FYL	1226	NPT			1092	KBS	296	SEL	1688	GHD
891	NPT	1227	PMN	17	NPT	1097	WVJ	299	SDN	1689	WHL
917	NPT	1228	MID	32	CAR	1117	DAR	301	BOR	1690	BOR
938	NPT	1229	FYL	45	CAR	1119	NEV	304	WHL	1735	WHL
1001	NPT	1230	PMN	61	SDN	1133	KBS	317	TDK	1758	YK
1003	TDK	1231	SKN	79	BOR	1135	DAR	326	TDK	1789	SBK
1004	BOR	1256	PMN	81	DAR	1154	DAR	338	GHD	1796	BOR
1005	NPT	1393	TDK	90	NPT	1158	NPT	347	HLA	1797	DAR
1006	PMN	1402	SUN	100	SUN	1164	YK	399	YK	1831	YK
1007	NPT	1686	FYL	116	DAR	1297	BOR	400	HTN	1832	WHL
1008	NPT	2338	HTN	119	SBH	1299	NPT	401	WHL	1833	BOR
1010	NPT	2339	TDK	146	SUN	1333	DAR	402	TDK	1834	BOR
1011	PMN	2340	BOR	174	SKN	1412	YK	403	HTN	1835	NEV
1012	PMN	2341	BLA	175	NPT	1413	NEV	447	YK	1836	MID
1013	FYL	2342	YK	183	SUN	1418	FYL	448	HLD	1861	BLA
1014	PMN	2343	YK	196	BOR	1419	YK	449	DAR	1862	BOR
1015	SDN	2344	BOR	202	BOR	1421	FYL	450	WHL	1863	SUN
1016	PMN	2345	WHL	204	NPT	1425	KBS	451	HLA	1864	HLD
1017	PMN	2346	WHL	206	FYL	1429	BOR	452	DAR		
1018	PMN	2347	NPT	227	SUN	1450	BOR	453	CAR	**J72** (75)	
1022	PMN	2348	BOR	251	YK	1451	YK	478	TDK		
1023	PMN	2349	WHL	253	SEL	1453	SDN	482	BOR	462	HLD
1024	SUN	2350	WHL	282	HLD	1456	WHL	492	SBK	1715	HLD
1025	SBK	2351	NPT	292	PMN			493	HLA	1718	DAR
1027	PMN	2352	WHL	302	SEL	**J71** (119+1)		494	MID	1720	NMN
1028	FYL	2353	WHL	303	DUR			495	WHL	1721	HLD
1029	SDN	2354	YK	308	NPT	27	DAR	496	DAR	1722	GHD
1030	SUN	2355	YK	309	THK	50	SDN	499	HLA	1728	GHD
1034	PMN	2356	NPT	311	SUN	54	BOR	501	BOR	1732	HTN
1035	PMN	2357	NEV	325	NPT	70	BOR	533	WHL	1733	HTN
1036	SUN	2358	SDN	327	MAL	77	EHL	541	EHL	1734	HTN
1039	BLA	2359	SDN	330	SBK	84	EHL	572	HTN	1736	DAR
1040	PMN	2360	SDN	332	NMN	103	HTN	577	DAR	1741	GHD
1044	SBK	2361	SDN	339	HAWJ	137	EHL	584	TDK	1742	SKN
1046	PMN	2362	WHL	375	NEV	144	TDK	802	SDN	1744	DAR
1047	TDK			389	BOR	161	BLA	811	GHD	1746	YK
1048	SKN	**J28** (20)		391	BOR	165	MID	969	HTN	1747	HTN
1049	DAR			392	YK	168	DAR	972	EHL	1749	HTN
1050	TDK	3014	HLS	396	BOR	176	EHL	977	SDN	1761	DAR
1052	SUN	3016	HLS	397	NPT	177	BLA	978	DAR	1763	EHL
1053	SUN	3017	HLS	398	BOR	179	BOR	980	EHL	1770	EHL
1056	SUN	3019	HLS	417	BOR	181	BLA	1083	HLD	2173	WHL
1060	PMN	3020	HLS	421	SEL	221	GHD	1084	YK	2174	WHL
1061	SUN	3021	HLS	488	FYL	224	EHL	1085	YK	2175	WHL
1064	FYL	3022	CUD	600	DAR	225	HLA	1095	TDK	2176	WHL
1065	CAR	3024	HLS	608	SDN	237	YK	1103	DAR	2177	GHD
1066	FYL	3025	HLS	626	DAR	239	HLA	1123	HTN	2178	WHL
1067	CAR	3026	HLS	627	HAV	240	TDK	1134	YK	2179	WHL
1189	SDN	3028	HLS	636	MAL	241	SDN	1140	YK	2180	WHL
1201	NPT	3029	HLS	641	NPT	242	BLA	1142	PMN	2181	DAR
1203	NPT	3030	HLS	670	KBS	244	BLA	1143	EHL	2182	TDK
1204	SEL	3031	HLS	805	BOR	248	HTN	1144	HTN	2183	TDK
1205	PMN	3032	HLS	896	SUN	252	BLA	1151	WHL	2184	SUN
1211	SEL	3157	HLS	913	SBH	254	BOR	1153	EHL	2185	EHL
1212	SEL	3158	HLS	916	PMN	260	EHL	1155	HLD	2186	SUN
1213	NEV	3159	HLS	990	FYL	261	CAR	1157	NMN	2187	BOR
1214	MID	3160	HLS	991	CAR	263	DAR W	1163	YK	2188	BOR
1216	SEL	3161	HLS	1038	PMN	268	BLA	1167	YK	2189	BOR
1219	NPT			1041	FYL	272	BLA	1196	MID	2190	BOR
1220	NPT	**'1001'** (1)		1076	HLD	275	HTN	1197	SEL	2191	BOR
1221	SDN			1080	SDN	278	NEV	1198	SKN	2192	SDN
1222	SDN	1275	MAL	1082	NEV	280	HTN	1199	HLD	2303	MID
1224	FYL			1087	KBS	285	CAR	1314	EHL	2304	MID

2305 MID	3115 HLA	1021 DAR	238 CON	1648 ANP	**Q5** (90)
2306 MID	3116 HLA	1033 EHL	267 SBK	1649 HLS	
2307 YK	3142 HLS	1115 MID	271 HTN	1650 HLS	83 SDN
2308 HLD	3143 HLS	1116 NBH	284 HLD	1651 WAUK	130 HLD
2309 YK	3144 CUD	1313 NEV	287 HLD	1652 ANP	162 HAV
2310 MID	3145 CUD	1340 WHL	293 SUN	1653 HLS	410 NPT
2311 SUN	3146 CUD	1341 WHL	345 EHL	1654 EHL	411 HAV
2312 WHL	3147 HLS	1342 SUN	346 HLD	1655 EHL	430 NPT
2313 YK	3148 HLS	1343 NBH	348 BLA	1705 EHL	443 HLD
2314 SKN	3149 HLS	1344 TWD	349 BOW		444 SDN
2315 DAR	3150 HLS	1346 YK	350 WAS	**N10** (20)	474 NPT
2316 GHD	3151 HLS	1347 TWD	351 HLS		527 NPT
2317 HLD		1348 YK	371 SEL	89 HLD	578 HLS
2318 HLD	**J76** (10)	1349 HLD	373 HLD	429 NEV	642 SDN
2319 DAR		1430 NBH	428 WAS	1109 BLA	643 ANP
2320 HTN	124 FYL	1431 YK	445 SBK	1112 HLD	644 NBH
2321 TDK	171 HLA	1432 NPT	503 CAR	1132 NEV	645 HLD
2322 TDK	193 HLD	1433 HLD	504 HTN	1138 BOW	646 SDN
2323 SUN	197 NEV	1435 WHL	509 HLD	1148 SEL	647 SEL
2324 EHL	198 NEV	1438 TDK	515 HLD	1317 NEV	648 NPT
2325 BLA	211 NEV	1439 PMN	523 HLD	1321 GHD	650 NPT
2326 EHL	598 HLD	1460 THK	528 WAS	1667 ALN	651 EHL
2327 EHL	599 FYL	1461 HLD	531 HLD	1683 BOW	652 HLD
2328 YK	602 HLD	1462 NEV	535 HLD	1697 HLD	653 SDN
2329 DAR	1059 HLD		573 HLD	1706 HLD	654 BOR
2330 DAR		**J78** (1+1)	683 HLD	1707 SUN	655 ANP
2331 YK	**J77** (60)		780 SUN	1710 NEV	656 HLS
2332 YK		590 PMN	809 EHL	1711 HLD	657 SDN
2333 YK	15 NPT	995 GHD W	855 CAR	1716 GHD	658 SDN
2334 YK	37 TWD		856 CON	1774 HLD	659 NPT
2335 BLA	43 MID	**J79** (2+1)	857 TWD	1785 HLD	660 SKN
2336 BLA	47 SBH		858 SUN		661 SEL
2337 BLA	57 NBH	407 MID	859 SEL	**N11** (5)	669 HLD
	71 NEV	1662 GHD W	860 MAL		715 HLD
J73 (10)	105 MID	1787 MID	861 HLD	3097 HLS	764 HLS
	138 YK		862 HTN	3098 HLS	767 TDK
544 TDK	145 HLD	**J80** (3)	863 EHL	3099 HLS	769 EHL
545 FYL	151 NPT		864 HLD	3100 CUD	770 NBH
546 HTN	164 SBH	3067 HLS	959 HLD	3101 HLS	771 HLD
547 FYL	166 SBK	3068 HLS	961 EHL		772 SDN
548 FYL	173 WHL	3069 HLS	1072 BLA	**N12** (9)	773 HLD
549 PEL	199 HLD		1091 TWD		774 SDN
550 HTN	276 SBK	**'44'** (5)	1104 SKN	3102 CUD	781 SDN
551 PEL	290 TDK		1105 WAS	3103 CUD	783 EHL
552 TDK	305 MID	44 EHL	1124 HLD	3104 HLS	785 HLD
553 FYL	319 WHL	49 SUN	1127 GHD	3105 BCJ	789 NPT
	324 GHD	94 HTN	1145 SUN	3106 CUD	792 NPT
J74 (8)	333 SBH	98 SUN	1152 SEL	3107 BCJ	793 NBH
	344 MID	106 SDN	1165 SBK	3108 CUD	794 NPT
20 HLA	354 NPT		1168 WAS	3110 BCJ	939 SDN
64 HLA	597 SKN	**N8** (62)			1002 HLD
82 HLA	604 THK		**N9** (20)	**N13** (10)	1009 NPT
88 HLA	607 NPT	14 SUN			1031 NBH
461 HLA	612 SKN	74 HLD	383 EHL	3013 HLS	1032 HLS
467 HLA	614 SKN	76 HLD	1617 HLS	3015 HLS	1054 NBH
489 HLA	623 HLD	136 WAS	1618 DAR	3018 HLS	1062 HLD
662 HLA	948 HLD	185 WAS	1640 EHL	3023 CUD	1110 NPT
	953 EHL	210 HLD	1641 BCas	3027 HLS	1111 HAV
J75 (16)	954 NEV	212 SKN	1642 BCas	3152 CUD	1128 SKN
	956 SDN	213 NEV	1643 DAR	3153 HLS	1149 SCA
3111 HLS	958 BLA	215 HLD	1644 EHL	3154 HLS	1150 NPT
3112 HLS	998 NMN	216 HLD	1645 BLA	3155 HLS	1173 HLD
3113 HLA	999 YK	218 SBK	1646 WAUK	3156 HLS	1177 HLD
3114 HLS	1000 YK	219 HLD	1647 HLD		1178 NPT

1186	NPT	2216	NPT	2280	NEV	**X1** (1)	
1215	HLD	2217	HLD	2281	CAR		
1218	NPT	2218	HLD	2282	NEV	66	DAR
1320	NPT	2219	SEL	2283	SEL		
1669	NPT	2220	HLD	2284	SKN	**X2** (1)	
1682	HLD	2221	HLD	2285	SKN		
1684	NPT	2222	BLA	2286	SKN	957	HLB
1685	NPT	2223	TDK	2287	BOR		
1694	HLD	2224	SEL	2288	BOR	**X3** (1+1)	
1696	SDN	2225	TDK	2289	NPT		
1700	NPT	2226	SEL	2290	BOR	190	HTN
1704	NPT	2227	BOR	2291	BOR	1679	YK
1708	SBK	2228	SEL	2292	BOR		
1709	BOR	2229	TDK	2293	TDK	**Y7** (17+2)	
1717	SBK	2230	HLS	2294	BOR		
1729	SKN	2231	TDK	2295	BOR	24	HLA
1731	NPT	2232	TDK	2296	NPT	129	DAR W
1757	NPT	2233	HLD	2297	HLD	518	TDK
2116	ANP	2234	HLD	2298	NEV	519	HTN
2117	NPT	2235	SKN	2299	HLS	587	TDK
2118	SDN	2236	BOR	2300	BOR	898	DAR W
2119	SDN	2237	HLS	2301	HLD	900	HLA
2120	NPT	2238	BLA	2302	BOR	945	TDK
2121	NPT	2239	HLD			946	TDK
2122	NPT	2240	TDK			1302	HLA
2123	NPT	2241	HLD	**Q7** (5)		1303	TDK
2124	ANP	2242	TDK			1304	GHD
2125	SDN	2243	TDK	901	HLD	1306	TDK
		2244	HLD	902	HLD	1307	GHD
Q6 (120)		2245	TDK	903	TDK	1308	TDK
		2246	HLD	904	HLD	1310	TDK
1247	TDK	2247	BOR	905	HLD	1798	HLA
1248	SEL	2248	SKN			1799	HLA
1249	HLS	2249	HLD	**Q10** (15)		1800	GHD
1250	BOR	2250	HLD				
1251	BOR	2251	SEL	3117	HLS	**Y8** (5)	
1252	NPT	2252	HLD	3118	HLS		
1253	TDK	2253	SKN	3119	HLS	559	HLD
1254	TDK	2254	CAR	3120	HLS	560	HLD
1257	NEV	2255	TDK	3121	HLS	561	HLD
1261	NEV	2256	DAR	3122	HLS	562	HLD
1262	TDK	2257	CAR	3123	HLS	563	HLD
1264	TDK	2258	BLA	3124	HLS		
1271	DAR	2259	CAR	3125	HLS		
1276	SEL	2260	BLA	3126	HLS		
1278	TDK	2261	BLA	3127	HLS		
1279	TDK	2262	BLA	3128	HLS		
1280	HLS	2263	TDK	3129	HLS		
1283	SEL	2264	TDK	3130	HLS		
1284	TDK	2265	TDK	3131	HLS		
1285	TDK	2266	BLA				
1288	SEL	2267	BLA	**T1** (10)			
1291	TDK	2268	CAR				
1292	SEL	2269	BLA	1350	HLD		
1293	TDK	2270	HLD	1351	NPT		
1294	TDK	2271	CAR	1352	HLD		
1311	HLS	2272	HLD	1353	NPT		
1335	BOR	2273	SEL	1354	SEL		
1361	TDK	2274	SKN	1355	TDK		
1362	SEL	2275	TDK	1356	TDK		
1363	TDK	2276	TDK	1357	TDK		
2213	TDK	2277	HLS	1358	TDK		
2214	SEL	2278	HLD	1359	TDK		
2215	TDK	2279	BOR				

THE STATUS OF SUB-SHEDS

As already mentioned, the Great Northern only made specific allocation according to Districts, of which there was seven, six of them having sub-sheds. They were as follows:-

District No.	Name	Sub-sheds at:-
1	**Doncaster**	Retford, York
2	**New England**	Boston, Louth, Lincoln Sleaford
3	**King's Cross**	Hornsey, Hatfield, Hitchin, Cambridge
4	**Colwick**	Derby
5		d

frequently, but it is possible to assess how many were usually at each, from the shed layout and the duties for which it was responsible. So the distribution at 1/1/23 could well have been:-

Bethnal Green	3	Millwall	6
Bishops Stortford	6	North Woolwich	1
Brentwood	8	Ongar	3
Buntingford	3	Palace Gates	10
Canning Town	2	Romford	1
Chelmsford	2	Southend-on-Sea	20
Enfield Town	14	Southminster	2
Epping	7	Wickford	3
Hertford	10	Wood Street	19
Ilford	26		

giving a total of 146 out-stationed from Stratford.

eld as Halifax; single engine, icester never ngines stayed ermine which

because, on ts allocation, s, of which it mine which s were made

The other main Great Eastern sheds of Cambridge, Norwich, and Ipswich all had a number of sub-sheds, as did the other Companies in the Group, but it was only on the North Eastern where a sub-shed was given a nominated allocation, a couple of which well merit being mentioned. Pateley Bridge (sub of Starbeck) just had a single engine for working the six daily weekday trains on the 14½ miles to and from Harrogate. At 1st January 1923 it was 0-4-4 tank no.1839, which was still their allocation on 31st December 1947, although by then re-numbered to 7253. Such consistency was not limited to passenger engines, because at Bowes Bridge (sub to Gateshead) 0-6-2 goods tank no.1138 was there throughout the full 25 years of the LNER, although by the LAST DAY you had to look for it as no.9100.

Kittybrewster shed housed all the 0-4-4 tank engines used for working the Aberdeen suburban services, no.87 being one of them.

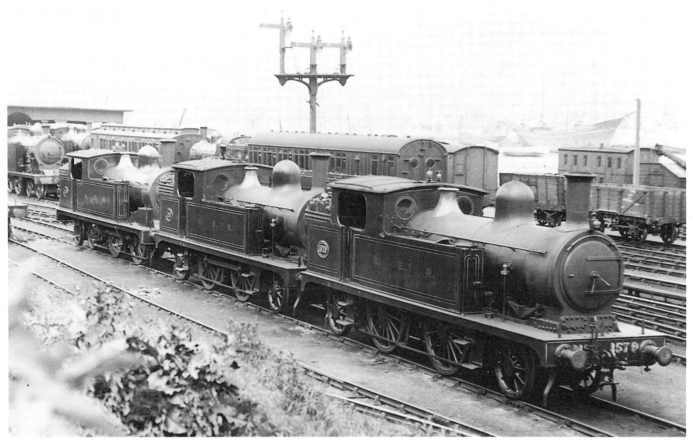

Whitby shed yard in June 1923 with three of the resident tank engines awaiting further duties. F8 no.1579 heads the line-up. *W.L.Good.*

On 1st January 1923 all the GC 4-6-2 tank engines, LNER class A5, were based at Neasden shed for working the outer suburban services from Marylebone. By the summer, no.447 had gained its new owners initials L.&N.E.R. on its tank sides and it is seen as such on Neasden shed yard. Later its number would have 5000 added along with all the other ex-Great Central engines.

For their Duplicate Stock, the North British numbered them from 1001 upwards, no.111 changing to 1406 in June 1921. For some time after Grouping it was still carrying that number both in large painted figures on the tank and by a cast brass plate on the bunker.

When ex-North British numbers took the LNER's 9000 addition, five-figure numbers resulted and they proved long lasting, as this photograph of 10406 was taken in its St Margarets shed on 9th September 1932. *L.Hanson.*

GREAT CENTRAL SHEDS

ANNESLEY (80)
B8 - 4, 279, 440/1/6 *(5)*
C14 - 1122/4/7/8/9 *(5)*
D9 - 1016/22/3/5/8/33/5/8/9 *(9)*
D12 - 428в, 442в, 443в *(3)*
12A - 169в *(1)*
J10 - 796, 816/35/49/50 *(5)*
J11 - 227/43/4/92/4, 302/6/26-9 *(11)*
J59 - 421в *(1)*
L1 - 273/4, 337/43/5/70 *(6)*
N5 - 764/5/7/70/4/5, 927/30/7/9 *(10)*
O4 - 271, 351/75/80/7/9, 408, 1212-21/3/4-8, 1238 *(24)*

BARNSLEY (43)
D7 - 710 *(1)*
J10 - 671 *(1)*
J13 - 570 *(1)*
N4 - 514, 613/23/9/30/4, 714/8/9/24/5 *(11)*
N5 - 21/5, 54, 127/89, 200/51, 515/21/33/44/6, 747/8/9/52/4/8/60/1/3/6 *(22)*
Q4 - 56/9, 68, 87, 91, 137/42 *(7)*

BIDSTON (7)
J58 - 8в, 72в, 156в *(3)*
J62 - 882/4/6/92 *(4)*

CHESTER (12)
C13 - 2, 9, 47, 55, 193, 310, 457 *(7)*
N5 - 751/6, 914/33/44 *(5)*

GORTON (178)
B1 - 195 *(1)*
B2 - 423-8 *(6)*
B3 - 1164-9 *(6)*
B5 - 185 *(1)*
B6 - 52, 53, 416 *(3)*
B7 - 34/5, 72/3/8, 470-4 *(10)*
B8 - 280, 439/42-5 *(6)*
B9 - 1106/9/10/13/14 *(5)*
D10 - 430/1/3-6/8 *(7)*
D12 - 425в, 434в *(2)*
F1 - 574-7/80/2-5/7/8/9/94/5/6, 726-37 *(27)*
F2 - 776/84 *(2)*
'18' - 309в *(1)*
J9 - 648/51/9/64 *(4)*
J10 - 134, 848 *(2)*
J11 - 202/8/10/11/24/5/6/32/4-7/42/5/7/55/89, 290/1, 303/13/6/9, 951/5/91/3, 1003/4/78 *(30)*
J58 - 22в, 52в, 53в *(3)*
J59 - 275в, 276в, 420в *(3)*
L1 - 275 *(1)*
N5 - 518/9/20/2-9/32/4-7/40-3/8, 896, 900/5, 932/40, 943/6 *(28)*
O4 - 1, 5, 8, 26, 93, 102/55, 334/52-5/77/8/9, 393-6, 412/3, 966, 1183, 1234/9 *(25)*
O5 - 420/2 *(2)*
Q4 - 92, 1052, 1134 *(3)*

IMMINGHAM (101)
B1 - 196 *(1)*
B5 - 180-4 *(5)*
B7 - 36/7/8 *(3)*
D7 - 561/6/7, 682/5/6/7, 708 *(8)*
D9 - 1018 *(1)*
J10 - 786/97, 800/5/6/17/9/37/8/40/1/4/6 *(13)*

IMMINGHAM *cont*
J11 - 973-90/2/4-9, 1000/1/2/5-8/10/11/12 *(35)*
J58 - 41в *(1)*
J59 - 272в, 273в, 279в, 280в, 367в, 414в, 415в *(7)*
J61 - 407в, 278 *(2)*
J62 - 885/7/9 *(3)*
J63 - 60, 61, 277, 321 *(4)*
L1 - 272 *(1)*
O4 - 403, 1203/4/37/42-5/8/9/50/2 *(12)*
Q4 - 144, 964, 1181 *(3)*
Y2 - 62в, 63в *(2)*

KEADBY (19)
O4 - 1206/40 *(2)*
Q4 - 39, 57, 63, 85, 139/40/3/7/50/3/60/2, 956, 1074/6, 1144/78 *(17)*

LANGWITH (61)
C14 - 1120/1/3 *(3)*
G3 - 1148в-1152в, 1169в *(6)*
J11 - 204/17/8/22/3/9/39/40/6/56/7/88, 312/7, 318, 948, 1080 *(17)*
J58 - 66в *(1)*
J60 - 1153в-1156в *(4)*
L1 - 340/66 *(2)*
M1 - 1146 *(1)*
N4 - 621 *(1)*
N6 - 1145в, 1147в, 40/2/3, 1154/5/6/9/62 *(10)*
Q4 - 957/9, 1077, 1132/3/5-43/76/9 *(16)*

LEICESTER (26)
B7 - 31/2/3 *(3)*
C4 - 192, 264-7, 358/60/1/3, 1083/6/7/9/90, 1092 *(15)*
C5 - 258/9, 364/5 *(4)*
J11 - 203/5 *(2)*
N5 - 923/6 *(2)*

LINCOLN (36)
B5 - 187 *(1)*
B9 - 1105/7/8/11/12 *(5)*
D7 - 562/4, 700/5 *(4)*
D9 - 113, 1013/21/4/36 *(5)*
E2 - 507в, 509в *(2)*
J11 - 177, 220/48/53/93/9, 300/8/11/4/5/22, 1009, 1115/6/8 *(16)*
J58 - 88в, 154в *(2)*
N4 - 620 *(1)*

LIVERPOOL (BRUNSWICK) (54)
D6 - 268/70, 859/62/3/4/9/71/7-81 *(13)*
D9 - 110, 1017 *(2)*
D12 - 423в, 430в, 446в *(3)*
F2 - 777-82/5 *(7)*
J10 - 90/4-7, 101/18/41/72/4/5/6, 807/10 *(14)*
J11 - 307 *(1)*
J59 - 336в, 371в, 418в *(3)*
J63 - 157, 538 *(2)*
N5 - 895, 904/11/22/4/5 *(6)*
X4 - 968/70/2 *(3)*

LIVERPOOL (WALTON) (33)
C4 - 1085 *(1)*
D5 - 694-9 *(6)*
D6 - 269 *(1)*
D8 - 508в, 510в, 511в *(3)*
E2 - 506в *(1)*

LIVERPOOL (WALTON) *cont*
F2 - 783 *(1)*
J10 - 76/9-84, 99, 100/3/23/5 *(12)*
J12 - 505в *(1)*
J59 - 368в, 374в *(2)*
N5 - 908/18/21/36/41 *(5)*

MEXBOROUGH (170)
B5 - 186, 1067-72 *(7)*
C13 - 199, 1064 *(2)*
D7 - 563, 688-92 *(6)*
D9 - 112 *(1)*
J10 - 74, 75, 77 *(3)*
J11 - 206, 309 *(2)*
J12 - 7в, 30в, 31в, 32в, 34в, 35в, 38в, 458/60, 462в, 463/5/7/8в, 475/6/7/81/5/6-92/4 *(27)*
J13 - 568/9/71/2/3 *(5)*
J59 - 274в, 277в, 413в, 417в *(4)*
N4 - 723 *(1)*
N5 - 51, 173, 516/7/45/7, 744/6/50/3/5/7/9/62, 769 *(15)*
O4 - 69, 133, 331/2/3/5/46-50/76/84/6/8/90/1/2, 197, 398, 400/2/4-7, 1184-1202/7-10/22/41 *(51)*
O5 - 10-13, 417/21 *(6)*
Q4 - 44, 48, 49, 58, 62/4/5/7, 135/6/45/6/8/49, 151/2/9/63/4, 356, 401, 958/60/1/2/3/5, 1053/4, 1073/5, 1174/5/7/80/2 *(36)*
S1 - 1170-3 *(4)*

NEASDEN (69)
A5 - 23, 24, 128/9/65-70, 371-4, 411/47-52 *(21)*
B7 - 458-61/3/4 *(6)*
C14 - 1125 *(1)*
D10 - 429/32/7 *(3)*
D11 - 501-11 *(11)*
E8 - 449в, 450в *(2)*
J11 - 221/50/82/5/98, 1081/2 *(7)*
J58 - 158в *(1)*
J59 - 372в *(1)*
L1 - 276, 336/9/41/2/67 *(6)*
N5 - 745/72/3, 894/7, 913/7/34/42/5 *(10)*

NEW HOLLAND (10)
D7 - 684, 706/11 *(3)*
D12 - 128в, 439в *(2)*
J10 - 808/9/23/7 *(4)*
J63 - 89 *(1)*

NORTHWICH (35)
D7 - 701-4/7/9 *(6)*
J9 - 645/6/7/9/50/2-8/60-3/5-9, 738-43 *(27)*
J10 - 641/4 *(2)*

RETFORD (44)
C13 - 1058 *(1)*
D9 - 104/5/7 *(3)*
J10 - 787/9/90-5/9, 802/13/8/21/2/8/31/2/45/7 851 *(20)*
J11 - 230/1/49/54/83/4/6/7/95/6, 304/24, 1079, 1117/9 *(15)*
J58 - 73в *(1)*
O5 - 414/5/8/9 *(4)*

SHEFFIELD (108)
B4 - 1095-1104 *(10)*
B7 - 465/6 *(2)*
C13 - 1055/6/7/9-63/5/6 *(10)*
D7 - 565, 683/93 *(3)*

SHEFFIELD cont

D9 - 106/8/9/11, 1014/5/9/20/6/7/9/30/1/2/4, 1037/40/1/2 *(19)*

J10 - 639/40/2/3/70/2/3-81, 814 *(16)*

J11 - 16, 301/5/30, 947/9/50/3/4 *(9)*

J59 - 340B, 370B *(2)*

N4 - 601/2/4-8/11/2/7/9/22/6/7/8/31/2/3/8, 716/21/2 *(22)*

O4 - 381/2/3/5/99, 1205/46/7 *(8)*

O5 - 14, 15, 17, 19, 22 *(5)*

Q4 - 70, 213 *(2)*

STAVELEY (47)

D12 - 440B *(1)*

J8 - 549-60 *(12)*

J62 - 890 *(1)*

N4 - 512/3, 603/9/10/4/5/6/8/24/5/35/6/7, 712, 713/5/7/20 *(19)*

O4 - 1211/29-33/5/6/51 *(9)*

Q4 - 71, 86, 138/61, 212 *(5)*

STOCKPORT (47)

C13 - 20 *(1)*

C14 - 1130/1 *(2)*

F1 - 578/9/81/6/90-3/7/8/9, 600 *(12)*

J10 - 98, 116/7/9-22/4/6/30/1/2, 820/4/5/6/9, 830/3/4/6/9/43 *(23)*

J59 - 338B, 339B, 342B *(3)*

N5 - 907/9/10/12/15/31 *(6)*

TRAFFORD PARK (63)

C13 - 18, 27, 29, 50, 114/79/91, 357, 456 *(9)*

D6 - 852-8/60/1/5-8/70/2-6 *(19)*

D12 - 441B *(1)*

J10 - 788/98, 801/3/4/11/12/15 *(8)*

J11 - 952, 1045 *(2)*

J12 - 36B, 37B, 45B, 459B, 461B, 464B, 466B, 469B, 470B, 478/9/84/93/7/8/9, 500, 503B *(18)*

J58 - 5B *(1)*

N5 - 768, 919 *(2)*

X4 - 967/9/71 *(3)*

TUXFORD (16)

M1 - 1145/7-53 *(8)*

N6 - 1146B, 41, 66, 1157/8/60/1/3 *(8)*

WIGAN (15)

J12 - 3B, 6B, 46B, 471B-474B, 480/2/3/95/6, 501B, 502B, 504B *(15)*

WOODFORD (48)

B7 - 462/7/8/9 *(4)*

C4 - 194, 260-3, 362, 1084/8/91/3/4 *(11)*

C14 - 1126 *(1)*

J11 - 197/8, 201/7/9/14/5/6/9/28/33/8/41/52, 281/97, 320/3/5, 1043/4/6-51 *(27)*

L1 - 338/44/68/9 *(4)*

N5 - 771 *(1)*

WREXHAM (36)

C13 - 28, 115/71/8/88/90, 359, 453/4/5 *(10)*

J10 - 842 *(1)*

J58 - 78B *(1)*

J62 - 883/8/91/3 *(4)*

'7' - 10B, 11B *(2)*

N5 - 409/10, 530/1/9, 898/9, 901/2/3/6/16/20, 928/9/35/8 *(17)*

WMCQ - 400B *(1)*

GREAT EASTERN GROUP

CAMBRIDGE (178)

B12 - 1504/7/12/14/20/1/2/4/6/7/8/30 *(12)*

D13 - 704/12/28/42/79, 1012/5/6/21/3/31, 1035/6 *(13)*

D14 - 1876/92/3 *(3)*

D15 - 1790/2/7, 1802/8/11/12/4/6/23/33/40, 1889/90/1/4 *(16)*

E4 - 417/30/2/3/6/8/54-7/9/60/3/79, 500/1, 502/4 *(18)*

F3 - 1061/3/85 *(3)*

F4 - 799 *(1)*

F7 - 1302/7/8/10 *(4)*

J15 - 508-11/20/6/7/9-32/5/6/48/9/53/63/70/1, 646, 805/6/25/6/31-40/2/3/5/8/9/51/6/7/97, 908/20/1/8/9 *(48)*

J16 - 1171/2/5-83/90/1/9 *(14)*

J17 - 1173/4/89/93/8, 1236 *(6)*

J18 - 1245/6 *(2)*

J19 - 1251/2/4/65/7/8/9 *(7)*

J20 - 1270/2/3/4/82/3/4/6/7/8/94 *(11)*

J65 - 151/2 *(2)*

J66 - 291/8, 307/18 *(4)*

J67 - 11, 12, 199, 330/97/9, 404/5 *(8)*

J68 - 27 *(1)*

J69 - 162/98, 273, 362 *(4)*

J70 - 131 *(1)*

COLCHESTER (47)

D13 - 733/4/9/44/5/8/56 *(7)*

D14 - 1867/71 *(2)*

D15 - 1813/46/55/97 *(4)*

E4 - 473 *(1)*

F3 - 1046/67/9/76 *(4)*

F4 - 146/9 *(2)*

F5 - 141 *(1)*

F7 - 1300/1 *(2)*

J14 - 951/9/76/7/8 *(5)*

J15 - 539/40/1/67, 600/42/90-3, 924-7 *(14)*

J66 - 293 *(1)*

J67 - 327/34 *(2)*

J69 - 364 *(1)*

Y5 - 231 *(1)*

DONCASTER (5)

D13 - 700, 1020/32 *(3)*

D15 - 1899 *(1)*

E4 - 483 *(1)*

IPSWICH (131)

B12 - 1500-3/5/15/8/9/23/9/35/7-40/52, 1561-6 *(22)*

D13 - 731/7/8/41/65 *(5)*

D14 - 1868/70/3 *(3)*

D15 - 1803/6/7/15/20/1/2/32/41/2/58/9/69 1874/82/8 *(16)*

E4 - 413/21/2/5/65-71/4/81/98 *(14)*

F3 - 1064/5/6/8/70-3/7 *(9)*

F4 - 665 *(1)*

F5 - 144/7 *(2)*

J14 - 984 *(1)*

J15 - 37/8/9, 525/37/8/45/6/59/66/8/9/92-9, 641/94, 914/33/4/6/7/9-43 *(32)*

J65 - 245/6/7/52/4 *(5)*

J66 - 292/5/6/7, 315/22/3 *(7)*

J67 - 13, 16, 333/6 *(4)*

J69 - 55, 335/84 *(3)*

IPSWICH cont

J70 - 125/6/7/9/30/5/9 *(7)*

KING'S LYNN (37)

D13 - 718, 1018 *(2)*

D15 - 1794, 1896 *(2)*

E4 - 418/9/24/37/44/58/62/4/76/7/8/80/2, 503 *(14)*

F3 - 1044/82/4 *(3)*

J14 - 970/3 *(2)*

J15 - 625, 801/2/41/7 *(5)*

J66 - 287/90, 301/8/9 *(5)*

J67 - 169, 398, 402/3 *(4)*

LINCOLN (12)

D13 - 1025/8/39 *(3)*

J15 - 523/8, 618 *(3)*

J16 - 1187 *(1)*

J17 - 1231/3 *(2)*

J66 - 282/99, 300 *(3)*

LOWESTOFT (22)

D14 - 1881 *(1)*

E4 - 449/53/93 *(3)*

F3 - 1089/94-8 *(6)*

F4 - 654/78 *(2)*

J15 - 119/21/2/4, 613/31, 812 *(7)*

J65 - 159 *(1)*

J66 - 326 *(1)*

Y5 - 209 *(Dept' 1)*

MARCH (97)

D13 - 706/17/29/51/77, 1029 *(6)*

D14 - 1895 *(1)*

D15 - 1810/24/30/5 *(4)*

E4 - 441/84, 505/6 *(4)*

J14 - 993 *(1)*

J15 - 512/8/21/2/4/33, 627/8/80-3/5/9, 803/46/90 *(17)*

J16 - 1184/5/6/8/92/5/6 *(7)*

J17 - 1194/7, 1223-30/2/4/7/8/9 *(15)*

J18 - 1241-4/7/8/9 *(7)*

J19 - 1250/3/60-4/6 *(8)*

J20 - 1271/5-81/5/9/90-3 *(14)*

J66 - 275-80/3/4/9, 319 *(10)*

J67 - 406 *(1)*

J68 - 28 *(1)*

J69 - 328 *(1)*

NORWICH (119)

B12 - 1509/10/3/6/7/67-70 *(9)*

D13 - 707/66/7, 1037 *(4)*

D14 - 1877/8/9 *(3)*

D15 - 1809/25/6/7/31/6/45/63/83/4/5/7 *(12)*

E4 - 420/3/6/8/9/39/40/2/3/5-8/50/1/2/72/5/85, 486/7/90/1/2/4/5/6 *(27)*

F3 - 1045/7/8/9/78/9/86/7/8/91/2/3/9 *(13)*

F4 - 666/77 *(2)*

J14 - 998 *(1)*

J15 - 120, 543/4/62/4/5, 609-12/14-7/20/9/30/3, 634/8/9, 807/9/10/13/5/6-20/4/8/9/30/66 *(36)*

J16 - 1168 *(1)*

J17 - 1210 *(1)*

J65 - 154 *(1)*

J66 - 314/7/20/5 *(4)*

J67 - 161/4 *(2)*

J69 - 163/7/90 *(3)*

PARKESTON (20)
B12 - 1508/11/32/6 *(4)*
D13 - 735 *(1)*
D15 - 1839/44/98 *(3)*
F3 - 1042/74/5 *(3)*
F4 - 148 *(1)*
J14 - 983 *(1)*
J15 - 944/5 *(2)*
J65 - 150, 248/50/1/3 *(5)*

PETERBOROUGH EAST (86)
D13 - 704/5/10/13/9/32/72/5, 1030 *(9)*
E4 - 434/5/99 *(3)*
J14 - 963 *(1)*
J15 - 547, 621/84/6/8, 821/7/54/8/9, 919/30, 931 *(13)*
J16 - 1150/1/2/4/5/7-67, 1200/3-6/8/9 *(23)*
J17 - 1153/6/69/70, 1201/2/7/11-22 *(19)*
J19 - 1140-9 *(10)*
J66 - 285, 313/21 *(3)*
J67 - 400/1 *(2)*
J68 - 29, 30 *(2)*
J69 - 191 *(1)*

STRATFORD (555)
B12 - 1523/31/3/4/41-51/3-60 *(23)*
D13 - 1026/7/33 *(3)*
D14 - 1862/4/5/6/72/5/86, 1900 *(8)*
D15 - 1791/3/5/6/8/9, 1804/5/17/8/9/28/9/34, 1838/47-54/6/7/60/1 *(27)*
E4 - 407-12/4/5/6/27/31/61 *(12)*
F3 - 1040/1/3/60/2/80/1/3 *(8)*
F4 - 71-80, 92/3/7/8/9, 101/2/5/6/7/11/40, 171-8/80-7/9, 211-25/32-44, 572-88/91, 650/3, 655/7/9/60/2/3/8/9/70/4/5/6/9, 791-8, 800*(109)*
F5 - 91/4/5/6, 100/3/4/8/9/10/42/3/5/70/9/88, 589/90, 780-8 *(27)*
F6 - 1-10, 61-70, 789/90 *(22)*
F7 - 1303-6/9/11 *(6)*
G4 - 1100-39 *(40)*
J14 - 604, 980/1/5/7 *(5)*
J15 - 507/14-7/9/34/50-4/6/7/8/60/1, 622/3, 640/3/4/5/7/8/9/96-9, 823/44/50/2/3/5/60-5, 867-81/3/6-9/91-6/8/9, 900-7/9-13/15-8/22/3, 932/8 *(91)*
J17 - 1235 *(1)*
J18 - 1240 *(1)*
J65 - 153/5-8, 249 *(6)*
J66 - 286/8/94, 302/3/4/10/11/12/16/24 *(11)*
J67 - 14, 15, 17-20, 200-8/55-64, 329/31, 332 *(28)*
J68 - 21-26, 41-50 *(16)*
J69 - 51-4/6-60, 81-90, 165/6/8/92-7, 265 266-72/4, 305/37-61/3/5-83/5-96 *(95)*
N7 - 1000-11 *(12)*
Y4 - 226-9 *(4)*

STRATFORD WORKS (Departmentals 7)
J66 - 281 *(1)*
J92 - B, C, D *(3)*
Y4 - 210 *(1)*
Y5 - 0228, 230 *(2)*

WISBECH (7)
J70 - 136 *(1)*
Y6 - 0125/6/9, 132/3/4 *(6)*

YARMOUTH (20)
D13 - 730, 1013 *(2)*
D15 - 1800/1/37/43/80 *(5)*
E4 - 488/9/97 *(3)*
F3 - 1090 *(1)*
J14 - 964 *(1)*
J15 - 542, 635/6, 814 *(4)*
J69 - 160 *(1)*
J70 - 128/37/8 *(3)*

GREAT NORTHERN GROUP

ARDSLEY (94)
C12 - 1019, 1528/39/42 *(4)*
D3 - 1302 *(1)*
J3 - 388/99 *(2)*
J4 - 147ᴀ, 175ᴀ, 187, 307/23/31/6/49/54/71/8, 718/9/29/34/44/99, 850, 1012/44/86, 1101, 1171 *(23)*
J6 - 547/59/60 *(3)*
J7 - 374, 1027/8/9 *(4)*
J50 - 221-30 *(10)*
J51 - 157/8/60/1/3/7/8/9/71/3/5/6/8, 211/12, 213/5-20 *(22)*
J52 - 977, 1207/26/83/4 *(5)*
J53 - 928/68/78, 1052 *(4)*
J54 - 679 *(1)*
K1 - 1634 *(1)*
K2 - 1640/8/52/8/75/6 *(6)*
Q1 - 413/9/28/44/5 *(5)*
Q2 - 405/6/7 *(3)*

BOSTON (62)
C12 - 1504/9/10/18 *(4)*
D2 - 45, 1367/71/9/80/2/4/94/5 *(9)*
D3 - 1343/50/7/9 *(4)*
D4 - 1356/8/60 *(3)*
E1 - 753/5/8, 885, 994/5/8/9, 1061/4/8 *(11)*
G1 - 943 *(1)*
J1 - 13, 14, 15 *(3)*
J2 - 73 *(1)*
J4 - 191/5, 832/45, 1032/83, 1106/45 *(8)*
J6 - 571/2/82/95/9, 600/2/4/33/4 *(10)*
J54 - 153ᴀ, 692, 781/8, 856, 907 *(6)*
J55 - 620, 790 *(2)*

BRADFORD (90)
C12 - 1009ᴀ, 1013/5/7/8/20, 1536/40/3-7, 1549 *(14)*
D3 - 1301/11 *(2)*
G1 - 766, 827, 932 *(3)*
G2 - 682/95 *(2)*
J1 - 5, 6, 8, 9 *(4)*
J2 - 71, 80 *(2)*
J3 - 1146/7 *(2)*
J4 - 102, 150ᴀ, 170ᴀ, 365/72/98, 640ᴀ, 750/97, 848, 1084/90/7/8, 1122/50/3 *(17)*
J7 - 1030 *(1)*
J51 - 159/62/4/6/70/4 *(6)*
J53 - 929/30/62/7/80, 1053 *(6)*
J54 - 494, 633ᴀ, 634ᴀ, 681, 804/5/8/53, 903/4/12/14 *(12)*
J55 - 397, 496, 636ᴀ, 677, 802/9/54, 913/6 *(9)*
N1 - 1554/60/4/8/72/4/93/4/5 *(10)*

CAMBRIDGE (10)
C1 - 1411/28 *(2)*
C2 - 252/3/4, 949 *(4)*

CAMBRIDGE cont
D1 - 56, 60/1/2 *(4)*

COLWICK (231)
C12 - 1511/5/7/9/20/3/4/6/30 *(9)*
D2 - 1327/9/61/3/4/73/5/93/9 *(9)*
D3 - 400, 1305/6/9/10/15-18/20/53/4/5 *(13)*
E1 - 760, 818/64/97, 992 *(5)*
G1 - 769, 824/8/30, 940 *(5)*
J1 - 4 *(1)*
J2 - 76/7/8 *(3)*
J3 - 177, 303/6/8/16/43/79, 1091/4/6, 1113/5/9/20/41/2/51/61-5/8 *(23)*
J4 - 165/79/99, 318/29/34/48/52/61/96, 721, 849, 1031/3/4/5/40/1/95, 1111/2/6/7/43/4/66 *(26)*
J5 - 27, 30, 33 *(3)*
J6 - 521/2/4-8/40-5/9-52/7/8/61-6/73-7/80/1/3, 587/8, 601/26-30 *(41)*
J7 - 156ᴀ, 188, 1021/3/4 *(5)*
J52 - 1208/59/60 *(3)*
J53 - 965/6, 1055 *(3)*
J54 - 673/80/9/90, 906/20 *(6)*
J55 - 672/4/8, 851, 917/8 *(6)*
J56 - 613 *(1)*
K1 - 1630/3/8/9 *(4)*
K2 - 1631/5 *(2)*
O1 - 464/9/70/1 *(4)*
Q1 - 401/8/9/11/12/4/5/8/25/6/7/36/7/9, 443/8/9 *(17)*
Q2 - 402/10/6/7/21/50/1 *(7)*
R1 - 116/8-24/6-36/8-50/2/3/5 *(35)*

COPLEY HILL (43)
C12 - 1010/4, 1501/31/2/5/8 *(7)*
D1 - 51-55 *(5)*
D2 - 43, 44, 1326/76 *(4)*
D3 - 1075/6 *(2)*
G2 - 659/94/6 *(3)*
J3 - 1152 *(1)*
J4 - 135ᴀ, 182, 840/3, 1011/43, 1140/72 *(8)*
J51 - 172, 214 *(2)*
J53 - 963 *(1)*
J54 - 858/9/60, 902 *(4)*
J55 - 806/10, 915 *(3)*
N1 - 1556/66/92 *(3)*

DONCASTER (189)
A1 - 1470/1 *(2)*
C1 - 251/72/3/6/80/95/8, 300, 1419/20/2-5/34, 1435/6/48/9/51-6 *(25)*
C2 - 250/60/71, 986 *(4)*
D2 - 1325/8/34/5/62/78/86/7/96/7/8 *(11)*
D3 - 1341/2/5/7/8/9 *(6)*
J2 - 79 *(1)*
J3 - 344/51/62/81/6, 1045, 1123/4/6/7/8/32/3/4, 1156/7/9/73 *(18)*
J4 - 180/92, 315/45/53/68, 725/6/46/8, 833/8/9, 846, 1118/25/9/31/5/49/54/5/8/60 *(24)*
J5 - 21, 25, 26, 29, 35, 37 *(6)*
J6 - 533/5/46/56/67/70/90/1/8, 606-10/31/2, 635-40 *(22)*
J52 - 1201/2/3/36-9/41-50/8/64/6/71/2/86/7, 1288 *(25)*
J53 - 155ᴀ, 924/73, 1049 *(4)*
J54 - 637ᴀ, 688, 780/4, 801/7/52, 911 *(8)*
J55 - 779/82/3/7, 803 *(5)*
J56 - 611 *(1)*
J57 - 140ᴀ *(1)*

DONCASTER cont
K2 - 1642/50/7/9/70/2/3/7/8/85-94 *(19)*
K3 - 1004/5/6 *(3)*
Q1 - 403/38 *(2)*
Q2 - 453/5 *(2)*

GRANTHAM (67)
C1 - 275/81-7/93/4/6/7, 1401-6/14-8/30-3/46, 1447/57 *(30)*
C2 - 1525/7/9/33 *(4)*
D1 - 57, 58, 59 *(3)*
D2 - 1332/8/9/74 *(4)*
D4 - 1077/9 *(2)*
E1 - 715, 812/61/8/82/4/93 *(7)*
J3 - 1114 *(1)*
J4 - 304/32, 1092/3, 1107 *(5)*
J5 - 38, 39, 40 *(3)*
J6 - 523/9/30 *(3)*
J52 - 1210 *(1)*
J54 - 619, 635A, 905 *(3)*
J57 - 134A *(1)*

HATFIELD (29)
C12 - 1502/12/14/34/7/41/8/50 *(8)*
D2 - 1377 *(1)*
D3 - 1078 *(1)*
G1 - 767/70 *(2)*
J1 - 1, 2, 3, 11 *(4)*
J3 - 384, 1100/69 *(3)*
J4 - 101 *(1)*
J54 - 855, 901/9 *(3)*
N1 - 190 *(1)*
N2 - 1759-63 *(5)*

HITCHIN (28)
D2 - 49, 50, 1336/7/85/8/9 *(7)*
D3 - 1072/3/80 *(3)*
J1 - 7, 10 *(2)*
J3 - 342/87, 1099, 1137/9 *(5)*
J4 - 313/4, 641, 716, 1037/88 *(6)*
J6 - 539/85 *(2)*
J54 - 675 *(1)*
J57 - 149A *(1)*
N2 - 1764 *(1)*

HORNSEY (76)
J3 - 1136/70 *(2)*
J4 - 383, 844, 1036, 1138 *(4)*
J52 - 970, 1060, 1227-35/51/2/4/6/7/85 *(17)*
J53 - 921/2/3/5/6/7/64/9/71/2/4/5/6/9, 1046/7, 1048/50/1/4/6-9 *(24)*
N1 - 1551/2/3/5/7/8/9/61/2/5/71/3/5-8/80/4/5, 1586/8/91/8 *(23)*
N2 - 1751-5/68 *(6)*

KING'S CROSS (156)
C1 - 274/7/8/9/99, 301, 1400/27/8/40-4/50, 1458-61 *(19)*
D2 - 41, 42, 1321/2/33/40/66/91 *(8)*
D3 - 1312/14/46 *(3)*
J1 - 12 *(1)*
J3 - 717 *(1)*
J4 - 302/73, 642, 745, 834 *(5)*
J6 - 584/92 *(2)*
J52 - 1204/40/53/5/61/2/75/81/2 *(9)*
J53 - 111, 961, 1212-15 *(6)*
J54 - 139A, 676, 785/6, 857, 910 *(6)*
J55 - 473A *(1)*

KING'S CROSS cont
J56 - 612/15 *(2)*
J57 - 144A, 684-7 *(5)*
K1 - 1632 *(1)*
K2 - 1645/9/51/3-6/66-9/71/4/9 *(14)*
K3 - 1008/9 *(2)*
N1 - 1563/7/70/9/81/2/3/9/96/7/9, 1600-5 *(17)*
N2 - 1606-15, 1721-50/6/7/8/65/6/7/9/70 *(48)*
R1 - 117/25/37/51/4/6 *(6)*

LEICESTER (5)
D2 - 1365 *(1)*
D3 - 1319/52 *(2)*
J3 - 375 *(1)*
J5 - 28 *(1)*

LINCOLN (32)
C12 - 1016 *(1)*
D2 - 46, 1368/9/92 *(4)*
D3 - 1303 *(1)*
D4 - 1313 *(1)*
E1 - 867/83/7, 1062/3/7/9 *(7)*
J3 - 1109 *(1)*
J4 - 317/94, 644, 730/1, 1039/81/5, 1110 *(9)*
J52 - 1217/76 *(2)*
J54 - 617/91, 908 *(3)*
J55 - 610A, 638A *(2)*
J56 - 608A *(1)*

LOUTH (8)
C12 - 1503/6/13 *(3)*
D2 - 1383 *(1)*
D3 - 1304/7 *(2)*
E1 - 814, 1000A *(2)*

NEW ENGLAND (180)
C1 - 288-92, 1300, 1407-10/12/13/21/9/37/8, 1439/45 *(18)*
C2 - 255-9, 982/5/7-90 *(11)*
C12 - 1505/7/8/16/21/2 *(6)*
D1 - 63/4/5 *(3)*
G1 - 939 *(1)*
G2 - 765 *(1)*
J2 - 72/4/5 *(3)*
J3 - 390, 1082, 1103/4/5/8 *(6)*
J4 - 181/93/8, 312/39/85/92, 727, 1087, 1102 *(10)*
J6 - 531/2/4/48/54/5/78/9/89/93/4/6/7, 603/5, 621-5 *(20)*
J52 - 1209/16/18-25/67-70/7-80/9/90 *(20)*
J53 - 1211 *(1)*
J54 - 789 *(1)*
K1 - 1636/7 *(2)*
K2 - 1641/3/4/6/7/60-5/80-4/95-1704 *(26)*
K3 - 1000-3/7 *(5)*
O1 - 456-60/2/3/5-8/72-6 *(16)*
O2 - 461/77-86 *(11)*
Q1 - 404/22/3/4/9-35/40/1/2/6/7 *(16)*
Q2 - 452/4 *(2)*
Q3 - 420 *(1)*

RETFORD (30)
D2 - 1324/70/81 *(3)*
D3 - 1074, 1344 *(2)*
E1 - 993, 1070 *(2)*
J3 - 350, 1130/67 *(3)*
J4 - 196, 337/8/59, 643/6/8, 724/92/3, 831/7, 1121 *(13)*

RETFORD cont
J5 - 22/3/4/31/2/4/6 *(7)*

MANCHESTER (TRAFFORD PARK) (15)
J6 - 536/7/8/53/68/9/86 *(7)*
J52 - 1205/6/63/5/73/4 *(6)*
J54 - 693, 919 *(2)*

YORK (14)
C2 - 950/83/4 *(3)*
D2 - 47, 48, 1180, 1323/30/1/72/90 *(8)*
D3 - 1071, 1308/51 *(3)*

Departmentals (Not LNER Classified)
470A Hall Hills, Boston
533A Doncaster Works

GREAT NORTH OF SCOTLAND GROUP

ELGIN (14)
D39 - 3 *(1)*
D40 - 54 *(1)*
D41 - 95, 101, 109, 112 *(4)*
D42 - 4, 17 *(2)*
D44 - 63, 65 *(2)*
D45 - 51, 53, 58, 62 *(4)*

KEITH (14)
D39 - 2 *(1)*
D40 - 26, 27, 29, 113 *(4)*
D41 - 22, 23, 78, 80, 94, 99, 105 *(7)*
D42 - 9 *(1)*
D48 - 71 *(1)*

KITTYBREWSTER (94)
D38 - 75, 76, 77 *(3)*
D39 - 1 *(1)*
D40 - 25, 28, 31/3-6, 45-50, 52, 114/5 *(16)*
D41 - 19, 20/1/4, 79, 81/2/3, 93/6/7/8, 100/2/3, 104/6/7/8/10/11 *(21)*
D42 - 7, 10, 18, 72/3/4 *(6)*
D43 - 12, 13, 14 *(3)*
D44 - 64/6/7/8 *(4)*
D45 - 40, 57/9/60/1 *(5)*
D46 - 5, 6 *(2)*
D47 - 44A, 45A, 48A, 49A, 50A, 52A, 54A, 55, 56 *(9)*
D48 - 69, 70 *(2)*
G10 - 84-92 *(9)*
J90 - 8, 11, 15, 16, 39, 42 *(6)*
J91 - 37, 38, 41 *(3)*
Z4 - 43, 44 *(2)*
Z5 - 30, 32 *(2)*

NORTH BRITISH GROUP

ABERDEEN (19)
C11 - 870/1/2 *(3)*
D29 - 340 *(1)*
D31 - 739 *(1)*
J34 - 554, 1413 *(2)*
J36 - 707 *(1)*
J37 - 13, 136, 292/5, 460/1/76/85/6 *(9)*
N15 - 49, 70 *(2)*

BATHGATE (59)
D31 - 575/8, 639 *(3)*
D35 - 1452 *(1)*

BATHGATE cont
D50 - 1392 *(1)*
D51 - 1405/57 *(2)*
J31 - 1138 *(1)*
J33 - 137/40 *(2)*
J34 - 27, 28, 125/38, 530/4/8/64, 1380/1, 1409/18/9/31/72/7/9 *(17)*
J35 - 201/4/53, 374/8/81 *(6)*
J36 - 181/2, 250, 615/26/30/53/4/66/71/83/90, 709/10/16/23 *(16)*
N15 - 29, 97, 107, 386/98/9, 921-4 *(10)*

BERWICK (27)
D32 - 887/8/92 *(3)*
D33 - 865 *(1)*
E7 - 1245/6/56 *(3)*
J31 - 1134/95 *(2)*
J35 - 191, 206 *(2)*
J37 - 46, 123, 274, 301/2/5/13/4, 435/62/66, 480/91 *(13)*
J82 - 1333/51 *(2)*
N15 - 911 *(1)*

BLAYDON (N.E.) (2)
D31 - 312 *(1)*
J37 - 161 *(1)*

BURNTISLAND (30)
D51 - 1471 *(1)*
E7 - 1249 *(1)*
J31 - 1122/88 *(2)*
J33 - 21, 148/78 *(3)*
J34 - 30, 163, 529/33/41/51/61, 1420/74 *(9)*
J36 - 616/43/77/82, 762/94 *(6)*
J88 - 117/9, 836/7/9 *(5)*
N15 - 61, 65, 914 *(3)*

CARLISLE (CANAL) (39)
C10 - 905/6 *(2)*
C11 - 878-81 *(4)*
D29 - 360 *(1)*
D30 - 412/27 *(2)*
D31 - 36, 216/8 *(3)*
G7 - 93 *(1)*
J31 - 1132, 1221/4 *(3)*
J32 - 1311 *(1)*
J33 - 570/3 *(2)*
J34 - 1430 *(1)*
J35 - 186/9, 220/6, 367 *(5)*
J36 - 607/25/91 *(3)*
J37 - 101, 222, 436/54/5/8/9 *(7)*
J82 - 1348/9 *(2)*
J83 - 802/10 *(2)*

DUNFERMLINE (51)
C15 - 15, 26 *(2)*
D25 - 593 *(1)*
D31 - 262, 640/1 *(3)*
D35 - 1434 *(1)*
D51 - 1458 *(1)*
E7 - 1239/47 *(2)*
G7 - 92, 94 *(2)*
J31 - 1162/6/89, 1223 *(4)*
J33 - 112/59 *(2)*
J34 - 540/58/9/60, 1367/93/7, 1432/78 *(9)*
J35 - 120/93/6, 855 *(4)*
J36 - 145/76/83, 248, 628/61/2/81, 771 *(9)*
J37 - 162/7, 402 *(3)*

DUNFERMLINE cont
J82 - 1335 *(1)*
J83 - 812/31 *(2)*
N15 - 389/90, 917/8 *(4)*
Y9 - 40 *(1)*

DUNDEE (78)
C10 - 902 *(1)*
C11 - 509, 868/9 *(3)*
D25 - 598 *(1)*
D26 - 322/7 *(2)*
D29 - 245, 359/62, 896 *(4)*
D30 - 419-22/5 *(5)*
D31 - 765 *(1)*
D32 - 885/6 *(2)*
D33 - 382, 866 *(2)*
D34 - 505 *(1)*
D50 - 1391 *(1)*
D51 - 1406/65 *(2)*
G8 - 1320/5/34/8 *(4)*
G9 - 349-52/5 *(5)*
J34 - 543/53 *(2)*
J35 - 58, 194/5/7/8, 207/8/28/54, 335/7/64, 370/6 *(14)*
J36 - 179, 609/17/8/49/75, 751/74/6/8 *(10)*
J37 - 110/11, 296, 315, 430/1/77/9/89, 517 *(10)*
J83 - 805/8/15/19 *(4)*
J88 - 87 *(1)*
Y9 - 1084/92/8 *(3)*

EASTFIELD (181)
C15 - 6, 122/31/55, 265 *(5)*
C16 - 439/41/2, 513-6 *(7)*
D25 - 594, 600/2/3 *(4)*
D27 - 1321 *(1)*
D28 - 1322/88 *(2)*
D30 - 410/11, 497-501 *(7)*
D31 - 217/93, 638, 768 *(4)*
D33 - 332 *(1)*
D34 - 100/53, 221/41/2/56/8/81/98, 307, 405-8/90/3-6 *(19)*
D35 - 1442/8/9/53 *(4)*
D50 - 1390 *(1)*
D51 - 1429/54 *(2)*
G7 - 590 *(1)*
J31 - 1140 *(1)*
J32 - 1344/5/6 *(3)*
J33 - 170 *(1)*
J34 - 531/5/9/63, 1364/6/77/83/6, 1414 *(10)*
J35 - 57, 127/85, 202, 329/30/72, 849/56, 857 *(10)*
J36 - 247/80, 604/31/45/51/2/5/63/5, 706/21, 743/4/9/50/2/61/83/4/7 *(21)*
J37 - 8, 33, 44, 62, 98, 103/13/71/5, 260/3/72, 273/97/9, 300/3/6, 401/3/32/4/7/56/63/5, 506, 507/8/18 *(30)*
J82 - 1306/31/52/4 *(4)*
J83 - 800/18/21/3/9/32/3/4 *(8)*
J85 - 1168 *(1)*
J88 - 130/52, 234/7/90 *(5)*
N14 - 858-62 *(5)*
N15 - 69, 142/54/65/6, 223/4/9/51/9/76/82, 392, 453, 920/6 *(16)*
Y9 - 50, 144, 308/10, 547, 610, 1087/96 *(8)*

HAWICK (21)
D25 - 599 *(1)*

HAWICK cont
D29 - 898 *(1)*
D31 - 404, 576, 633 *(3)*
D51 - 1462 *(1)*
G7 - 90 *(1)*
J31 - 1133/7/47/8/9/80 *(6)*
J32 - 1300 *(1)*
J33 - 566/9 *(2)*
J34 - 544/56 *(2)*
J36 - 605, 742/6 *(3)*

HEXHAM (N.E.) (1)
J36 - 724 *(1)*

HAYMARKET (50)
C11 - 873-7 *(5)*
C15 - 1, 25, 141 *(3)*
D25 - 595/6/7 *(3)*
D27 - 1323/4 *(2)*
D28 - 1361/87 *(2)*
D29 - 338/9/61 *(3)*
D30 - 413-6/24/8 *(6)*
D31 - 211/2, 579, 642, 729/30/3-6 *(10)*
D34 - 291 *(1)*
D35 - 1439 *(1)*
J31 - 1070 *(1)*
J32 - 1314/15/43 *(3)*
J34 - 565 *(1)*
J35 - 373, 848 *(2)*
J82 - 1336 *(1)*
J83 - 813/26/8 *(3)*
J88 - 277, 844 *(2)*
N15 - 387 *(1)*

KIPPS (71)
C15 - 4, 267, 309 *(3)*
C16 - 438/46/7, 512 *(4)*
D51 - 1461/4 *(2)*
G7 - 586 *(1)*
G9 - 239, 475 *(2)*
J31 - 1164, 1208 *(2)*
J32 - 1298, 1312/37/9 *(4)*
J33 - 80, 150, 582-5 *(6)*
J34 - 532/6/48/57/62, 1368, 1407/12/75 *(9)*
J35 - 115, 377 *(2)*
J36 - 68. 180, 621/2/47/85/9, 714/8/55/60/3, 773 *(13)*
J37 - 468/87 *(2)*
J83 - 795-8 *(4)*
J84 - 1257 *(1)*
J88 - 121/32, 845 *(3)*
N15 - 257/64, 396/7, 919 *(5)*
Y9 - 11, 14, 63, 1088/91/3/4 *(7)*
Y10 - 1011 *(1)*

PARKHEAD (56)
C15 - 2, 3, 5, 16, 51, 64, 102/64 *(8)*
C16 - 440/3/4/5 *(4)*
D31 - 215 *(1)*
D36 - 695 *(1)*
G7 - 95, 588 *(2)*
G9 - 356 *(1)*
J31 - 1183, 1214 *(2)*
J32 - 1304/29 *(2)*
J33 - 83, 156, 484, 571 *(4)*
J34 - 18, 184, 482, 542/9/52, 1394, 1417 *(8)*
J35 - 371/80 *(2)*
J36 - 172/7, 623/73/4, 712/27/8/72 *(9)*

PARKHEAD *cont*
J37 - 457/64 *(2)*
J81 - 1216 *(1)*
J82 - 1328 *(1)*
J83 - 799, 814 *(2)*
J84 - 1259 *(1)*
J88 - 289, 842 *(2)*
N15 - 108, 240, 393 *(3)*

PERTH (24)
D29 - 243/4 *(2)*
D30 - 409/18 *(2)*
D31 - 214, 574, 634/7, 731/8 *(6)*
D34 - 270 *(1)*
D51 - 1463 *(1)*
G7 - 589 *(1)*
J34 - 1421 *(1)*
J35 - 56, 200 *(2)*
J36 - 668, 726 *(2)*
J37 - 478 *(1)*
J82 - 1330/53/6 *(3)*
J83 - 822 *(1)*
J88 - 843 *(1)*

POLMONT (45)
D51 - 1427/59/60 *(3)*
G7 - 587 *(1)*
J31 - 1190 *(1)*
J32 - 1297, 1305 *(2)*
J33 - 168/9, 580/1 *(4)*
J34 - 311, 537/45/50/5, 1396, 1481 *(7)*
J35 - 86, 203 *(2)*
J36 - 45, 606/11/44/6/57/69/86, 708/47/77 *(11)*
J37 - 261, 304, 433 *(3)*
J82 - 1289/94 *(2)*
J83 - 824 *(1)*
J86 - 1173 *(1)*
J88 - 840 *(1)*
N15 - 391, 925 *(2)*
Y9 - 9, 17, 32, 1103 *(4)*

REEDSMOUTH (5)
D51 - 1402 *(1)*
J33 - 24 *(1)*
J36 - 624, 754/79 *(3)*

ROTHBURY (2)
D51 - 1401 *(1)*
J36 - 791 *(1)*

STIRLING (25)
D25 - 592, 601 *(2)*
D31 - 37, 769 *(2)*
D51 - 1404/26/55 *(3)*
G7 - 591 *(1)*
G8 - 1326 *(1)*
G9 - 474 *(1)*
J31 - 1141/2/4, 1206 *(4)*
J34 - 1395, 1400 *(2)*
J35 - 348 *(1)*
J36 - 613/70, 741/5/64/92 *(6)*
J82 - 1299 *(1)*
J88 - 271 *(1)*

ST MARGARETS (213)
C10 - 901/3/4 *(3)*
C11 - 510 *(1)*
C15 - 12, 41/3/8, 53, 133/4/5 *(8)*

ST MARGARETS *cont*
C16 - 448-52, 511 *(6)*
D26 - 317/8/20/3-6 *(7)*
D29 - 895/7/9, 900 *(4)*
D30 - 363, 400/17/23/6 *(5)*
D31 - 213, 577, 732/7/40/66 *(6)*
D32 - 882/3/4/9/90/1 *(6)*
D33 - 331, 894 *(2)*
D34 - 266/78/87, 492, 502/3/4 *(7)*
D51 - 1411/24/5/8/56/66-70 *(10)*
G7 - 91 *(1)*
G8 - 1327 *(1)*
G9 - 334/53/4 *(3)*
J31 - 1082, 1143/6/78, 1200/27 *(6)*
J32 - 1319/41 *(2)*
J33 - 81/2/5, 249/69, 567/8/72 *(8)*
J34 - 286, 527, 1422/3 *(4)*
J35 - 59, 124/6/9/87/8/90/2/9, 205, 347/65/9, 379, 850/1/3/4 *(18)*
J36 - 358, 608/14/19/27/9/48/56/8/60/72/6/8, 679/80/4/7/8/92, 711/3/5/7/22/48/53/6-9/75/81, 782/6/8/9/90 *(37)*
J37 - 72/3, 84/8/9, 104/5/9/28/39/43/51/7/8, 255, 429/70-3 *(20)*
J82 - 1291, 1350/7/8 *(4)*
J83 - 801/3/7/16/7/25/7/30 *(8)*
J84 - 1270 *(1)*
J88 - 66, 114/6, 235/79/88, 841/6 *(8)*
N14 - 863 *(1)*
N15 - 7, 20, 22, 47, 54, 230/46/52, 388, 907-10/12 *(14)*
Y9 - 10, 42, 146, 546, 1083/9/90/5/7, 1100/1, 1102 *(12)*

THORNTON JUNCTION (75)
C15 - 39 *(1)*
D31 - 635/6, 767/70 *(4)*
D32 - 893 *(1)*
D33 - 333/83/4/5, 864/7 *(6)*
D34 - 34, 35, 149 *(3)*
J31 - 1114, 1296 *(2)*
J32 - 1310 *(1)*
J33 - 160 *(1)*
J34 - 481, 1365/9/70, 1410/5/6/73/6 *(9)*
J35 - 38, 336/66/8/75, 852 *(6)*
J36 - 173, 357, 612/20/32/50/9/64/7, 705/19, 720/5/80/5/93 *(16)*
J37 - 467/9/88 *(3)*
J82 - 1332/55/9 *(3)*
J83 - 804/6/9/11/20 *(5)*
J88 - 118, 233/6/8, 838/47 *(6)*
N15 - 96, 106, 209/10/19, 913/5/6 *(8)*

NORTH EASTERN GROUP

ALNMOUTH (11)
D17/1 - 1637 *(1)*
D22 - 18 *(1)*
E5 - 1478, 1504 *(2)*
'1440' - 220 *(1)*
F8 - 485, 1160 *(2)*
J21 - 1563, 1820 *(2)*
J22 - 565 *(1)*
N10 - 1667 *(1)*

ALSTON (1)
F8 - 35 *(1)*

ANNFIELD PLAIN (8)
J25 - 536, 1993 *(2)*
N9 - 1648/52 *(2)*
Q5 - 643/55, 2116/24 *(4)*

BARNARD CASTLE (8)
E5 - 1469 *(1)*
'901' - 269, 363/6/7, 464 *(5)*
N9 - 1641/2 *(2)*

BLAYDON (69)
B13 - 756/66/75 *(3)*
D20 - 2012 *(1)*
G5 - 1169, 1691, 1702/51/83, 1840/68 *(7)*
H1 - 1328/9/30, 1521/2 *(5)*
J21 - 315, 458, 965, 1122/88, 1301/37/8, 1557/64/88, 1607/9/10/11/3, 1812 *(17)*
J24 - 1854, 1934/55 *(3)*
J25 - 1985, 2137 *(2)*
J26 - 434, 1369 *(2)*
J27 - 1039, 2341 *(2)*
J71 - 161/77/81, 242/4/52/68/72, 1861 *(9)*
J72 - 2325/35/6/7 *(4)*
J77 - 958 *(1)*
N8 - 348, 1072 *(2)*
N9 - 1645 *(1)*
N10 - 1109 *(1)*
Q6 - 2222/38/58/60/1/2/6/7/9 *(9)*

BOROUGH GARDENS (65)
J22 - 522, 1481 *(2)*
J24 - 1828/41/98, 1900/37/8 *(6)*
J25 - 1986, 2000, 2133/41 *(4)*
J26 - 835/81 *(2)*
J27 - 1004, 2340/4/8 *(4)*
'398' - 79, 196, 202, 389/91/6/8, 417, 805, 1297, 1429/50 *(12)*
J71 - 54, 70, 179, 254, 301, 482, 501, 1690, 1796, 1833/4/62 *(12)*
J72 - 2187-91 *(5)*
Q5 - 654, 1709 *(2)*
Q6 - 1250/1, 1335, 2227/36/47/79/87/8/90, 2291/2/4/5, 2300/2 *(16)*

BOWES BRIDGE (3)
N8 - 349 *(1)*
N10 - 1138, 1683 *(2)*

BRADFORD (MANNINGHAM) (1)
D23 - 328 *(1)*

BRIDLINGTON (7)
D22 - 115/7, 230, 514, 684, 1536/9 *(7)*

BULLCROFT JUNCTION (4)
J23 - 3055 *(1)*
N12 - 3105/7/10 *(3)*

CARLISLE (LONDON ROAD) (49)
D17/2 - 1876, 1901/10/21/4/5/6/8/9 *(9)*
D22 - 154, 355, 1324 *(3)*
G5 - 2084/97 *(2)*
G6 - 60, 273, 322, 605/24 *(5)*
J21 - 104, 511/68/70, 666, 872, 1562, 1802, 1813 *(9)*
J25 - 257, 2075, 2140 *(3)*
J27 - 790, 839, 1065/7 *(4)*
'398' - 32, 45, 991 *(3)*

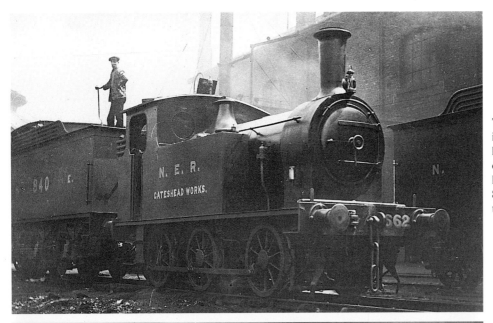

The North Eastern's Departmentals included this 0-6-0 tank engine, clearly labelled as to where it was assigned, and crane tank no.995 also had the same lettering. Two 0-4-0 tanks, nos. 129 and 898 carried DARLINGTON WORKS for their duties at that works.

For FIRST DAY, this Stratford Works 0-4-0 saddle tank does not qualify, because it had been withdrawn in 1921. But as B, C, and D became so well known, it was thought appropriate to show on what letter A had been carried.

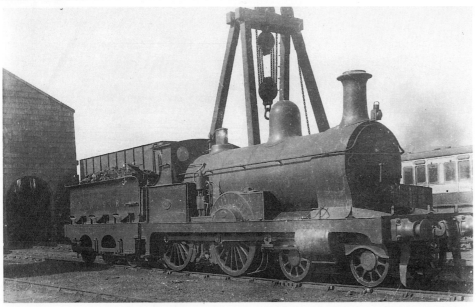

One of the oldest Great North of Scotland 4-4-0s, no.55 built in 1876, is here at its home shed of Kittybrewster.

By **FIRST DAY**, all surviving Hull & Barnsley engine numbers had been increased by 3000 to avoid confusion with similar N.E.R. numbers. 3077 here at Springhead had been changed by the works there in their normal style, tender lettering being ignored.

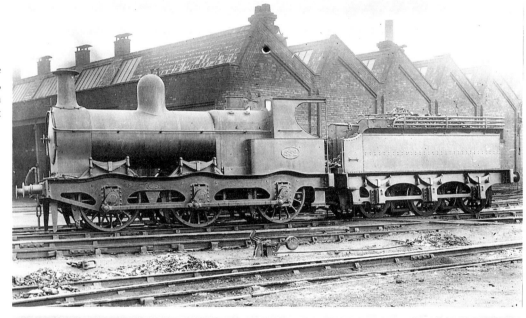

Great Central goods engine no.552 was at Staveley shed, where it was still to be seen when photographed on 16th August 1924.

At the western extremity of the North Eastern territory, no.2259 was at Carlisle (London Road) shed on FIRST DAY. Note that it still carries the distinctive Armstrong Whitworth makers plate on its leading sandbox.

CARLISLE (LONDON ROAD) cont
J71 - 261/85, 453 *(3)*
N8 - 503, 855 *(2)*
Q6 - 2254/7/9/68/71/81 *(6)*

CONSETT (2)
N8 - 238, 856 *(2)*

CUDWORTH (30)
J23 - 3049/50/1/3/6-9/70/1/5/81-8 *(19)*
J28 - 3022 *(1)*
J75 - 3144/5/6 *(3)*
N11 - 3100 *(1)*
N12 - 3102/3/6/8 *(4)*
N13 - 3023, 3152 *(2)*

DARLINGTON (83)
B15 - 824 *(1)*
D20 - 476, 1042, 1217, 2019/23, 2106/10 *(7)*
D23 - 372 *(1)*
E5 - 1463/7/70/4/5 *(5)*
'901' - 53 *(1)*
G5 - 468 *(1)*
H1 - 1327, 1502/3/24-7 *(7)*
J21 - 582, 611, 997, 1075, 1315, 1509/12/56, 1566/75/95 *(11)*
J22 - 502, 606, 1484/9 *(4)*
J24 - 1821/3/53/91, 1931/6/51 *(7)*
J25 - 1726, 1972/5, 2044/58 *(5)*
J26 - 1370 *(1)*
J27 - 1049 *(1)*
'398' - 81, 116, 600/26, 1117/35/54, 1333 *(8)*
J71 - 27, 168, 449/52/96, 577, 978, 1103, 1797 *(9)*
J72 - 1718/36/44/61, 2181, 2315/9/29/30 *(9)*
J77 - 1021 *(1)*
N9 - 1618/43 *(2)*
Q6 - 1271, 2256 *(2)*

DENABY (2)
J23 - 3080 *(1)*
N12 - 3108 *(1)*

DONCASTER (GN) (2)
B15 - 815 *(1)*
D17/1 - 1620 *(1)*

DURHAM (7)
'1440' - 1441/2/3/6/8 *(5)*
J22 - 1483 *(1)*
'398' - 303 *(1)*

EAST HARTLEPOOL (36)
J26 - 67, 1698 *(2)*
J71 - 77, 84, 137/76, 224/60, 541, 972/80, 1143/53, 1314 *(12)*
J72 - 1763/70, 2185, 2324/6/7 *(6)*
J77 - 953, 1033 *(2)*
'44' - 44 *(1)*
N8 - 345, 809/63, 961 *(4)*
N9 - 383, 1640/4/54/5, 1705 *(6)*
Q5 - 651, 769/83 *(3)*

FERRYHILL (28)
G5 - 427, 1882 *(2)*
J22 - 232, 620, 1102, 1490 *(4)*
J24 - 1827 *(1)*
J26 - 406 *(1)*

FERRYHILL cont
J27 - 888, 1013/28/64/6, 1224/9, 1686 *(8)*
'398' - 206, 488, 990, 1041, 1418/21 *(6)*
J73 - 545/7/8/53 *(4)*
J76 - 124, 599 *(2)*

GATESHEAD (104)
A2 - 2400/1 *(2)*
B14 - 2111-5 *(5)*
B16 - 920, 2363/5 *(3)*
C6 - 295, 696, 701/4/5, 1753/94 *(7)*
C7 - 706/9/16-22/7/8/9/32-7, 2170, 2205, 2209/12 *(22)*
C8 - 730/1 *(2)*
D17/1 - 1621/5/31/6/8 *(5)*
D17/2 - 1880, 1909/27 *(3)*
D20 - 1051, 1147/84, 1206/9/23/35/6/58 1665, 2016/30, 2105/7 *(14)*
D22 - 1546 *(1)*
F8 - 423, 804 *(2)*
G5 - 1788, 1916/20, 2093/5, 2100 *(6)*
G6 - 955 *(1)*
H1 - 1517, 2153-6 *(5)*
J21 - 51, 107, 259, 313, 1614, 1811/7/9 *(8)*
J25 - 1714, 2062 *(2)*
J71 - 221, 338, 811, 1688 *(4)*
J72 - 1722/8/41, 2177, 2316 *(5)*
J77 - 324 *(1)*
N8 - 1127 *(1)*
N10 - 1321, 1716 *(2)*
Y7 - 1304/7, 1800 *(3)*

GUISBOROUGH (1)
G6 - 1020 *(1)*

HAVERTON HILL (13)
F8 - 1598, 1606 *(2)*
J26 - 438, 1146/94, 1202/8, 1390, 1781 *(7)*
'398' - 627 *(1)*
Q5 - 162, 411, 1111 *(3)*

HAWES JUNCTION (2)
G6 - 588 *(1)*
'398' - 339 *(1)*

HAYMARKET (4)
C7 - 714, 2193/4, 2204 *(4)*

HEATON (130)
B13 - 752/7/9/61, 1077, 2002/3/5 *(8)*
B15 - 782/7/8/91/5-8, 825 *(9)*
B16 - 840-3/6, 906/14/22/30/2/4/7/43 *(13)*
C6 - 532, 649, 742/84, 1680, 1776 *(6)*
C7 - 710, 2195/6/7, 2200/3/6/11 *(8)*
D20 - 1078, 1207/32 *(3)*
G5 - 384, 1316, 1687, 1745/8/54/5/62/91/3, 1865/86, 1918, 2086/96 *(15)*
G6 - 62, 256, 323, 416 *(4)*
H1 - 1499, 1501/19/23/9, 2157-60 *(9)*
J21 - 31, 182, 360, 424/80, 513/38/9/58/69, 667, 871/7, 960/2/74/92/4, 1071, 1187, 1309, 1336, 1508/10/65/76, 1608, 1801/16/18 *(30)*
J26 - 342 *(1)*
J27 - 2338 *(1)*
J71 - 103, 248/75/80, 400/3, 572, 969, 1123/44 *(10)*
J72 - 1732/3/4/47/9, 2320 *(6)*
J73 - 546/50 *(2)*

HEATON cont
'44' - 94 *(1)*
N8 - 271, 504, 862 *(3)*
Y7 - 519 *(1)*

HEXHAM (5)
F8 - 1586 *(1)*
G5 - 405, 1765, 1867, 2094 *(4)*

HULL ALEXANDRA DOCK (24)
J71 - 225/39/86, 347, 451/93/9 *(7)*
J74 - 20, 64, 82, 88, 461/7/89, 662 *(8)*
J75 - 3113/5/6 *(3)*
J76 - 171 *(1)*
Y7 - 24, 900, 1302, 1798/9 *(5)*

HULL BOTANIC GARDENS (47)
D17/1 - 1622/3/6/8/9/30/3/5/9 *(9)*
D19 - 1619 *(1)*
D20 - 712, 1234, 2014, 2102/3 *(5)*
D22 - 42, 85, 96, 194, 340, 777, 803, 1137, 1534/40/3 *(11)*
D23 - 23, 222/3/58, 337, 521/57, 675/6/7/9 *(11)*
F8 - 187, 1322, 1582 *(3)*
G5 - 435/6, 1334, 1703 *(4)*
G6 - 247, 341 *(2)*
X2 - 957 *(1)*

HULL DAIRYCOATES (146)
A7 - 1126/75 *(2)*
B13 - 726/40/4/6/8/9/51/5/8/60/3/8, 2004/9, 2010 *(15)*
B15 - 786 *(1)*
E5 - 1468 *(1)*
J21 - 86, 97, 102, 291/4, 316/31, 431, 665/80, 778, 810/74, 963/76/81/93, 1513/48/68/71/2/90, 1612, 1815 *(25)*
J22 - 422, 571 *(2)*
J25 - 2038/48 *(2)*
'398' - 282, 1076 *(2)*
J71 - 448, 1083, 1155/99, 1864 *(5)*
J72 - 462, 1715/21, 2308/17/8 *(6)*
J76 - 193, 598, 602, 1059 *(4)*
J77 - 145/99, 623, 948, 1349, 1433/61 *(7)*
N8 - 74, 76, 210/5/6/9/84/7, 346/73, 509/15/23, 531/5/73, 683, 861/4, 959, 1124 *(21)*
N9 - 1647 *(1)*
N10 - 89, 1112, 1697, 1706/11/74/85 *(7)*
Q5 - 130, 443, 645/52/69, 715/71/3/85, 1002/62, 1173/7, 1215, 1682/94 *(16)*
Q6 - 2217/8/20/1/33/4/9/41/4/6/9/50/2/70/2/8, 2297, 2301 *(18)*
Q7 - 901/2/4/5 *(4)*
T1 - 1350/2 *(2)*
Y8 - 559-63 *(5)*

HULL SPRINGHEAD (120)
D22 - 808, 1538 *(2)*
D24 - 3033/5/8/41/2 *(5)*
F8 - 262 *(1)*
J23 - 3052/4/60-6/72/3/4/6-9/89-96, 3132, 3133-41 *(34)*
J25 - 2047/51 *(2)*
J28 - 3014/6/7/9/20/1/4/5/6/8-32, 3157-61 *(19)*
J75 - 3111/2/4/42/3/7-51 *(10)*
J80 - 3067/8/9 *(3)*
N8 - 351 *(1)*
N9 - 1617/49/50/3 *(4)*

HULL SPRINGHEAD cont
N11 - 3097/8/9, 3101 *(4)*
N12 - 3104 *(1)*
N13 - 3013/5/8/27, 3153-6 *(8)*
Q5 - 578, 656, 764, 1032 *(4)*
Q6 - 1249/80, 1311, 2230/7/77/99 *(7)*
Q10 - 3117-31 *(15)*

KIRKBY STEPHEN (14)
E5 - 1464/5/73 *(3)*
'901' - 1325 *(1)*
'1440' - 1449 *(1)*
J21 - 668, 800 *(2)*
J25 - 1966/94 *(2)*
'398' - 670, 1087/92, 1133, 1425 *(5)*

MALTON (18)
A6 - 695 *(1)*
D23 - 214 *(1)*
F8 - 201, 419, 1580/1 *(4)*
G5 - 394, 505 *(2)*
J22 - 235, 440, 506/8, 812, 1106 *(6)*
'1001' - 1275 *(1)*
'398' - 327, 636 *(2)*
N8 - 860 *(1)*

MASHAM (1)
F8 - 1599 *(1)*

MIDDLESBROUGH (62)
E5 - 1476, 1506 *(2)*
F8 - 420, 685, 854, 1597, 1601 *(5)*
G5 - 526, 1779/86/95, 1889 *(5)*
G6 - 65, 226, 343 *(3)*
J21 - 26, 68, 139/57, 289, 432, 1552/61/70/92, 1593/4, 1810 *(13)*
J24 - 1852/95/7, 1944/5/7/9/54/8/60 *(10)*
J25 - 463, 2041/80, 2130 *(4)*
J26 - 765 *(1)*
J27 - 1214/28 *(2)*
J71 - 165, 494, 1196, 1666, 1836 *(5)*
J72 - 2303-6/10 *(5)*
J77 - 43, 105, 305/44, 1115 *(5)*
J79 - 407, 1787 *(2)*

MIDDLETON-IN-TEESDALE (1)
'901' - 370 *(1)*

NEVILLE HILL (82)
A6 - 686 *(1)*
B13 - 743/50/3/62, 2006/8 *(6)*
B15 - 819 *(1)*
B16 - 929/31 *(2)*
C7 - 2201/7/10 *(3)*
D17/2 - 1875/7, 1905/23 *(4)*
D18 - 1869/70 *(2)*
D20 - 725, 2011/3/20/6, 2108/9 *(7)*
D21 - 1243/4 *(2)*
F8 - 72, 674, 801, 1584, 1602 *(5)*
G5 - 580, 1096, 1884 *(3)*
G6 - 108 *(1)*
H1 - 1326, 1518/31, 2143/7 *(5)*
J21 - 300, 619, 806, 1567/9/96, 1805/6/14 *(9)*
J25 - 1723, 1970/7, 2034/67 *(5)*
J26 - 543 *(1)*
J27 - 1213, 2357 *(2)*
'398' -375, 1082, 1119, 1413 *(4)*
J71 - 278, 1835 *(2)*

NEVILLE HILL cont
J76 - 197/8, 211 *(3)*
J77 - 71, 954, 1313, 1462 *(4)*
N8 - 213 *(1)*
N10 - 429, 1132, 1317, 1710 *(4)*
Q6 - 1257/61, 2280/2/98 *(5)*

NEWPORT (90)
J22 - 59, 131, 369, 1491 *(4)*
J24 - 1822/45/51/99, 1941/2/3/53/6/7 *(10)*
J25 - 1987, 2056, 2135 *(3)*
J26 - 1057, 1131/72, 1671/8, 1777 *(6)*
J27 - 814/91, 917/38, 1001/5/7/8/10, 1201/3, 1219/20/6, 2347/51/6 *(17)*
'398' - 17, 90, 175, 204, 308/25/97, 641, 1158, 1299 *(10)*
J77 - 15, 151, 354, 607, 1432 *(5)*
Q5 - 410/30/74, 527, 648/50/9, 789/92/4, 1009, 1110/50/78/86, 1218, 1320, 1669/84/5, 1700/4/31/57, 2117/20-3 *(29)*
Q6 - 1252, 2216/89/96 *(4)*
T1 - 1351/3 *(2)*

NORMANTON (4)
'398' - 332 *(1)*
J71 - 1157 *(1)*
J72 - 1720 *(1)*
J77 - 998 *(1)*

NORTHALLERTON (9)
F8 - 40, 279, 418/69, 1603 *(5)*
J24 - 1824/50 *(2)*
J25 - 2032/66 *(2)*

NORTH BLYTH (28)
F8 - 454, 575 *(2)*
G6 - 353, 952 *(2)*
J21 - 95, 122/33, 1616 *(4)*
J22 - 1482/7 *(2)*
J24 - 1843, 1933/40 *(3)*
J25 - 1961-4/8, 2063 *(6)*
J77 - 57, 1116, 1343, 1430 *(4)*
Q5 - 644, 770/93, 1031/54 *(5)*

PATELEY BRIDGE (1)
G5 - 1839 *(1)*

PELTON LEVEL (2)
J73 - 549/51 *(2)*

PENRITH (1)
'901' - 19 *(1)*

PERCY MAIN (33)
J22 - 1486 *(1)*
J24 - 1826/47/56 *(3)*
J25 - 2071, 2126/38 *(3)*
J26 - 379 *(1)*
J27 - 880, 1006/11/2/4/6/7/8/22/3/7/34/5, 1040/6/60, 1205/27/30/56 *(20)*
'398' - 292, 916, 1038 *(3)*
J71 - 1142 *(1)*
J77 - 1439 *(1)*

PICKERING (4)
G5 - 1888, 2088 *(2)*
G6 - 297 *(1)*
J22 - 192 *(1)*

RICHMOND (1)
G5 - 2089 *(1)*

ROSEDALE (3)
J24 - 1860/93, 1950 *(3)*

SALTBURN (16)
A6 - 687/90 *(2)*
E5 - 1477 *(1)*
G6 - 63, 91, 1055 *(3)*
H1 - 2144/5/6/8-52/62 *(9)*
J24 - 1849 *(1)*

SCARBOROUGH (27)
A6 - 693/4 *(2)*
B15 - 813 *(1)*
D17/2 - 1874/8, 1902/3/6/7 *(6)*
D22 - 356, 779, 1541/2 *(4)*
D23 - 217, 472, 1107 *(3)*
E5 - 1466/71 *(2)*
G5 - 381, 1701 *(2)*
G6 - 87 *(1)*
J22 - 497, 682, 1141 *(3)*
J25 - 2129/36 *(2)*
Q5 - 1149 *(1)*

SELBY (57)
A7 - 1126 *(1)*
D22 - 673, 1532/5/7/44 *(5)*
E5 - 1472 *(1)*
G6 - 189, 672 *(2)*
J21 - 973, 1554, 1808 *(3)*
J24 - 1894/6, 1948 *(3)*
J25 - 1974, 2035/6/7/49/50/2/5/7/70, 2128 *(11)*
J26 - 1159 *(1)*
J27 - 1204/11/12/16 *(4)*
'398' - 253, 302, 421 *(3)*
J71 - 296, 1197 *(2)*
N8 - 371, 859, 1152 *(3)*
N10 - 1148 *(1)*
Q5 - 647/61 *(2)*
Q6 - 1248/76/83/8/92, 1362, 2214/9/24/6/8/51, 2273/83 *(14)*
T1 - 1354 *(1)*

SHILDON (59)
A7 - 1129/74/80/3/95 *(5)*
G5 - 1737 *(1)*
J21 - 93, 99, 110, 944/96, 1323, 1507/50 *(8)*
J25 - 29, 1965, 2043/6/54/9, 2132/4 *(8)*
J27 - 1015/29, 1189, 1221/2/5, 2358-61 *(10)*
'398' - 61, 608, 1080, 1453 *(4)*
J71 - 50, 241/99, 802, 977 *(5)*
J72 - 2192 *(1)*
J77 - 956 *(1)*
'44' - 106 *(1)*
Q5 - 83, 444, 642/6/53/7/8, 772/4/81, 939, 1696, 2118/9/25 *(15)*

SOUTH BLYTH (28)
F8 - 169, 414, 507 *(3)*
G5 - 1883 *(1)*
G6 - 585/95, 947/50, 1436 *(5)*
J21 - 1161 *(1)*
J22 - 78, 681, 1488 *(3)*
J24 - 1830/42, 1932/5/59 *(5)*
J25 - 1969/71/6/98, 2064 *(5)*
'398' - 119, 913 *(2)*

SOUTH BLYTH cont
J77 - 47, 164, 333 *(3)*

STANHOPE (1)
G5 - 408 *(1)*

STARBECK (50)
A7 - 1170/82/5/93 *(4)*
D17/2 - 1922 *(1)*
D21 - 1242 *(1)*
D22 - 1533/45 *(2)*
D23 - 274, 678, 1120 *(3)*
G5 - 149, 439, 529, 1775, 1912/5, 2090/1, 2092 *(9)*
G6 - 334/58, 615 *(3)*
H1 - 1500/20/8/30, 2161 *(5)*
J21 - 22, 470, 510/56/79, 1549 *(6)*
J22 - 491 *(1)*
J26 - 517, 1773 *(2)*
J27 - 1025/44 *(2)*
'398' - 330 *(1)*
J71 - 492, 1789 *(2)*
J77 - 166, 276 *(2)*
N8 - 218/67, 445, 1165 *(4)*
Q5 - 1708/17 *(2)*

STOCKTON (47)
A7 - 1179/90 *(2)*
F8 - 205, 415 *(2)*
G5 - 1740/64, 1887/90, 2087 *(5)*
J21 - 30, 147/8, 209, 312, 520, 979, 1073, 1511/47/73/4/89 *(13)*
J22 - 1480 *(1)*
J24 - 1825/92 *(2)*
J25 - 459 *(1)*
J27 - 1048, 1231 *(2)*
'398' - 174 *(1)*
J71 - 1198 *(1)*
J72 - 1742, 2314 *(2)*
J77 - 597, 612/4 *(3)*
N8 - 212, 1104 *(2)*
Q5 - 660, 1128, 1729 *(3)*
Q6 - 2235/48/53/74/84/5/6 *(7)*

SUNDERLAND (81)
F8 - 128/55, 1578 *(3)*
G5 - 387, 437/41, 1692/3, 1730/52/9/69/72/8, 1837/85, 1917/9, 2081/3/98/9 *(19)*
G6 - 321, 465 *(2)*
J21 - 56, 101/60, 530, 776, 869/78, 1332, 1514/51 *(10)*
J24 - 1829/46/59, 1946 *(4)*
J25 - 1727, 1981/2/4/96/7, 2031/3/9/53/65, 2127 *(12)*
J27 - 836/83, 1024/30/6/52/3/6/61, 1402 *(10)*
'398' - 100/46/83, 227, 311, 896 *(6)*
J71 - 1863 *(1)*
J72 - 2184/6, 2311/23 *(4)*
J77 - 1342 *(1)*
'44' - 49, 98 *(2)*
N8 - 14, 293, 780, 858, 1145 *(5)*
N10 - 1699, 1707 *(2)*

THIRSK (14)
A7 - 1114/76 *(2)*
G5 - 1911 *(1)*
J21 - 1515 *(1)*
J25 - 1743, 1973/89/90/1, 2068, 2142 *(7)*

THIRSK cont
'398' - 309 *(1)*
J77 - 604, 1460 *(2)*

TWEEDMOUTH (44)
B13 - 738/9/41/5/7/54, 2001/7 *(8)*
B16 - 909/24/6/8 *(4)*
C6 - 697, 700/3 *(3)*
D17/1 - 1624/7/32/4 *(4)*
D20 - 592, 723, 1210, 2015/7/24/5/9 *(8)*
'1440' - 150 *(1)*
F8 - 21, 55, 425/83, 1604 *(5)*
G5 - 1838/66 *(2)*
J21 - 152, 1339, 1615 *(3)*
J22 - 455 *(1)*
J77 - 37, 1344/7 *(3)*
N8 - 857, 1091 *(2)*

TYNE DOCK (93)
F8 - 172, 404, 671, 1171, 1585, 1600/5 *(7)*
J21 - 123, 1559 *(2)*
J22 - 388 *(1)*
J24 - 1848/55/7/8, 1939 *(5)*
J25 - 1724/5, 1983, 2040/69/73/6/7 *(8)*
J26 - 555, 1676 *(2)*
J27 - 1003/47/50, 1393, 2339 *(5)*
J71 - 144,240, 317/26, 402/78, 584, 1095 *(8)*
J72 - 2182/3, 2321/2 *(4)*
J73 - 544/52 *(2)*
J77 - 290, 1438 *(2)*
Q5 - 767 *(1)*
Q6 - 1247/53/4/62/4/78/9/84/5/91/3/4, 1361/3, 2213/5/23/5/9/31/2/40/2/3/5/55/63/4/5/75/6, 2293 *(32)*
Q7 - 903 *(1)*
T1 - 1355-9 *(5)*
Y7 - 518/87, 945/6, 1303/6/8/10 *(8)*

WASKERLEY (9)
D22 - 663 *(1)*
J22 - 498 *(1)*
N8 - 136/85, 350, 428, 528, 1105/68 *(7)*

WEARHEAD (1)
G5 - 1881 *(1)*

WEAR VALLEY JUNCTION (4)
J21 - 1553 *(1)*
J25 - 25 *(1)*
'398' - 1090/7 *(2)*

WEST AUCKLAND (23)
F8 - 41 *(1)*
G6 - 949 *(1)*
J21 - 16 *(1)*
J22 - 567 *(1)*
J25 - 1967/78/9/80/8/92/5/9, 2042/5/61/72/4, 2078/9, 2131/9 *(17)*
N9 - 1646/51 *(2)*

WEST HARTLEPOOL (77)
A7 - 1181/91 *(2)*
D17/2 - 1871/2/3/9, 1904/8/30 *(7)*
E5 - 1505 *(1)*
G5 - 380, 413/33, 540, 1695, 1713/80, 1913, 2082/5 *(10)*
G6 - 92, 638, 1019 *(3)*
J21 - 48, 314, 564, 613, 875/6/99, 975, 1305,

WEST HARTLEPOOL cont
J21 cont - 1555/8/60/87/91 *(14)*
J22 - 446 *(1)*
J26 - 132, 233/43, 816, 1043, 1139, 1360, 1670/3 *(9)*
J27 - 2345/6/9/50/2/3/62 *(7)*
'398' - 1456 *(1)*
J71 - 304, 401/50/95, 533, 1151, 1689, 1735, 1832 *(9)*
J72 - 2173-6/8/9/80, 2312 *(8)*
J77 - 173, 319, 1340/1, 1435 *(5)*

WHITBY (17)
A6 - 688/9/91/2 *(4)*
F8 - 490, 537, 1577/9/83 *(5)*
G5 - 1319, 1739, 1914 *(3)*
J22 - 142, 208, 1485 *(3)*
J24 - 1952 *(1)*
J25 - 2060 *(1)*

YORK (129)
A7 - 1113/92 *(2)*
B15 - 799, 817/20-3 *(6)*
B16 - 844/5/7/8/9, 908/11/15/21/3/5/7/33/36/42, 2364 *(16)*
C6 - 698/9, 702, 1792 *(4)*
C7 - 2163-9/71/2/98/9, 2202/8 *(13)*
'38' - 281 *(1)*
D20 - 707/8/11/13/24, 1026, 1260, 1672, 2018/21/2/7/8, 2101/4 *(15)*
D21 - 1237-41/5/6 *(7)*
E5 - 1479 *(1)*
'901' - 910 *(1)*
'1440' - 486 *(1)*
G6 - 255/88, 466, 951, 1312 *(5)*
J21 - 34, 534, 807, 1516, 1803/4/7/9 *(8)*
J24 - 1844 *(1)*
J26 - 412/42, 525/54, 818/31, 1098, 1130, 1200, 1366, 1674 *(11)*
J27 - 2342/3/54/5 *(4)*
'398' - 251, 392, 1164, 1412/9/51 *(6)*
J71 - 237, 399, 447, 1084/5, 1134/40/63/67, 1758, 1831 *(11)*
J72 - 1746, 2307/9/13/28/31-4 *(9)*
J77 - 138, 999, 1000, 1346/8, 1431 *(6)*
X3 - 1679 *(1)*

Departmentals (8)

DARLINGTON (1)
X1 - 66 *(1)*

DARLINGTON WORKS (3)
J71 - 263 *(1)*
Y7 - 129, 898 *(2)*

GATESHEAD WORKS (2)
J78 - 995 *(1)*
J79 - 1662 *(1)*

HEATON (1)
X3 - 190 *(1)*

PERCY MAIN (1)
J78 - 590 *(1)*